WHAT ARE THEY SAYING ABOUT
THE LETTER TO THE HEBREWS?

What Are They Saying About the Letter to the Hebrews?

Daniel J. Harrington, SJ

PAULIST PRESS
New York/Mahwah, N.J.

Cover design by James Brisson
Book design by Theresa M. Sparacio

Library of Congress Cataloging-in-Publication Data

Harrington, Daniel J.
    What are they saying about the Letter to the Hebrews? / Daniel J. Harrington
       p.   cm. — (What are they saying about series)
    Includes bibliographical references.
    ISBN 0-8091-4320-8 (alk. paper)
    1. Bible. N.T. Hebrews—Chriticism, interpretation, etc. I. Title. II. WATSA series.

BS2775.52.H37 2005
227'.8706—dc22

                                  2004022087

Published by Paulist Press
997 Macarthur Boulevard
Mahwah, New Jersey 07430

www.paulistpress.com

Printed and bound in the
United States of America

Contents

1
Reading Hebrews Today

> "It was fitting that God, for whom and through whom all things exist, in bringing many children to glory, should make the pioneer of their salvation perfect through sufferings." (Heb 2:10)

The New Testament writing that is the subject of this book is often referred to as "Paul's Letter to the Hebrews." But everything about that statement is wrong. Hebrews is not a letter, nor does it address the Hebrews. It is a sermon in written form (see 13:22), and it originally addressed early Christians (most likely Jewish Christians). It was not written by Paul. Its language and theology are quite different from what we find in Paul's letters. We do not know exactly who the author was. In fact, the early Christian writer Origen said that "whoever wrote Hebrews, only God knows."

Hebrews is a long sermon. Indeed, it is arguably the greatest Christian sermon ever written down. It is a combination of biblical exposition and exhortation, which is exactly what a good sermon should be. Its language is sophisticated, and its doctrine is sometimes hard to grasp. But its content in the final analysis is simple. It explores in depth the theological significance of the early Christian confession of faith that "Christ died for our sins in accordance with the scriptures" (1 Cor 15:3). It portrays Jesus as both the perfect sacrifice for sins and the great high priest who willingly

1

offered himself as that sacrifice. It reflects on Jesus as God's Son and God's Word (1:1—4:13), his priesthood and sacrifice (4:14—10:18), and perseverance in Christian life (10:19—13:25).

The biblical quotation at the heading of this chapter (Heb 2:10) summarizes the central theme of Hebrews. What may be difficult to understand is the meaning of "perfect." Since elsewhere in Hebrews (4:15) the author insists that Christ did not sin, he cannot be talking about Christ's moral perfection. Rather, he must be talking about his functional or vocational perfection, about Christ being a perfect fit for his task. He was "perfect" for his mission, for what God wanted him to do for us.

In becoming human, Christ the Son of God became one of us, a flesh and blood human. Among the several things that characterize humans, one of the most prominent and universal is suffering. According to Hebrews, Christ showed his humanity especially in his suffering. Indeed his suffering was constitutive of his full humanity. It was precisely in his suffering that Christ proved himself to be our leader, the one who goes before us, the hero whom we follow, the liberator who leads us on to freedom.

The suffering that Jesus underwent was "for us" and "for our sins." His suffering was not only meaningful but even redemptive in the sense that it made possible a new relationship of intimacy and confidence with God. The early Christians addressed in Hebrews were apparently having an increasingly hard time in believing that their sins were really forgiven through Jesus' life, death, and exaltation. They had grown weary and even exhausted in their Christian confession, to the point that some were "neglecting to meet together" (10:25). In response to this crisis, the author of Hebrews appealed to the person of Jesus and his saving significance as the real answer to their spiritual weariness.

Hebrews is one of the more neglected writings in the New Testament. Its language is often difficult, and its conceptual world (especially its concern with sacrifice) is foreign to most people today. It appears in the Sunday cycles of lectionary readings only in short passages and without much context and so is generally ignored. Nevertheless, if we regard the saving significance of Jesus' life, death, and exaltation as the core of Christian faith, then we neglect Hebrews at our peril, since it is (with Paul's Letter to the Romans) the most sustained and sophisticated presentation of that core belief in the New Testament.

The survey of recent scholarship that follows treats books about Hebrews published since 1975. It seeks to inform prospective students of Hebrews about what is available to them by way of resources and to indicate where progress has been made in recent scholarship. After noting a few historical-critical and homiletical commentaries, it addresses work on some of the mysteries or "riddles" pertaining to Hebrews: its historical and intellectual background, religious and social setting, structure and other literary features, and authorship. Next it deals with its use of the "Old Testament": its hermeneutical stance, treatment of biblical figures, and use of specific biblical texts. Then it discusses the theology of Hebrews in general and some of its major themes: wandering and rest, priesthood and sacrifice, perfection, new covenant, sacred space, suffering, and faith. The books placed under each subsection are treated in the chronological order of their publication. My treatments are primarily descriptive, though I do make some critical comments where I deem them necessary.

Many of the books discussed here originated as doctoral dissertations, were published as technical monographs in prestigious academic series, and are found only in a few libraries specializing in theology. All the books are available in English, though a few translations have been included. Those who wish to move beyond English language publications should go to **Albert Vanhoye**'s *La Lettre aux Hébreux: Jésus Christ, médiateur d'une nouvelle alliance* (2001), and **Erich Grässer**'s three-volume *An die Hebräer* (1990–97). For important surveys of scholarship in German, see **Helmut Feld**'s *Der Hebräerbrief* (1985) and **Wolfgang Kraus**'s article in the journal *Verkündigung und Forschung* (2003). For an ongoing record of fifty years of scholarship on Hebrews in many languages, see *New Testament Abstracts*.

A few notes on terminology are in order here. Since we do not know the name of the author of Hebrews, I will generally refer to him (or her) as "the author of Hebrews" or simply "the author," not to be confused with the author of the book under discussion. Since Hebrews is best viewed as a sermon in written form, I use the traditional terms "letter" and "epistle" only sparingly. Since the author used the Greek version of the Bible and since he is more responsible than any other New Testament writer for our expression "Old Testament," I have avoided terms such as "Hebrew Scriptures" and "Jewish Bible" in favor of the traditional Christian nomenclature "Old Testament." And the "They" in this book's title refers to writings by competent biblical scholars over the last thirty years. My hope is that biblical scholars, theologians, students, pastors, and all who are interested in Hebrews will find what "They" are saying to be stimulating and enriching on the biblical, theological, and pastoral levels.

Reading Hebrews for the First Time

For those making a first step in the study of Hebrews, **Donald A. Hagner**'s *Encountering the Book of Hebrews* (2002) provides helpful guidance. Hagner, a well-known evangelical New Testament scholar, is the author of a substantial commentary on Hebrews (1983; rev. ed., 1990). He describes this volume as not a commentary but rather an exposition; that is, a tracing of the line of thought from section to section. His volume is part of a series intended for college-level Bible courses. The intellectual goals are to present the content of Hebrews, to introduce background information, to outline hermeneutical principles, to touch on critical issues, and to substantiate the Christian faith. The attitudinal goals are to make the Bible part of students' lives, to instill in students a love for the Scriptures, to make them better people, to enhance their piety, and to stimulate their love for God.

After treating introductory issues (origin and historical setting, structure, genre, etc.), Hagner offers a chapter-by-chapter exposition of Hebrews: (1) the most important thing God ever said; (2) the full humanity of the Son of God; (3) Christ is superior to Moses; (4) the remaining promises of rest; (5) the high priesthood of Christ; and so forth. Each chapter is introduced by a list of related biblical texts, a detailed outline of content, and three objectives. The expositions are accompanied by photographs and other illustrations, as well as many sidebars giving supplementary information. Each chapter concludes with study questions, a list of key terms, and bibliographical suggestions. Also included are an essay on the place of Hebrews in the New Testament and its contribution to theology, the church, and Christian life; an excursus on the entry of Hebrews into the New Testament canon; a select bibliography; a glossary of technical terms; and various indexes.

While written with evangelical Christian college students in mind, Hagner's exposition of Hebrews can serve as an excellent starting point for anyone studying Hebrews privately or in a group. It makes accessible to nonspecialist readers the best of modern scholarship on Hebrews and will whet their intellectual and theological appetites to delve more deeply into what is acknowledged as one of the most difficult books in the New Testament. It is a good example of effective biblical popularization for all who want to know more about Hebrews.

Full-Scale Commentaries

In treating the introductory issues pertaining to Hebrews, **Harold W. Attridge** in *Epistle to the Hebrews* (1989) in the Hermeneia commentary series exercises great caution, which he expresses in these words: "The beginning of sober exegesis is a recognition of the limits of historical knowledge" (p. 5). He is satisfied with describing Hebrews as an anonymous composition, dating it sometime between 60 and 100 CE and locating its addressees somewhere between Jerusalem and Rome. He regards Hebrews as a sermon or homily (an "epideictic oration"), adopts with some modifications the five-part outline proposed by Albert Vanhoye, and notes the author's emphases on fidelity ("let us hold fast") and on Christ the high priest as the key to the Old Testament. While acknowledging the many parallels with Philo's writings and some Qumran texts, Attridge maintains that "there is no single strand of Judaism that provides a clear and simple matrix within which to understand the thought of our author or his text" (p. 30). Likewise, with regard to early Christian traditions he finds no one decisive Christian affiliation, though he acknowledges links with Pauline and Johannine traditions as well as 1 Peter.

For each pericope Attridge supplies a title ("Exordium" for Hebrews 1:1-4), a fresh translation ("having spoken of old in multiple forms and multiple fashions to the fathers through the prophets," for 1:1), and textual notes (pertaining mainly to manuscript variant readings and textual emendations). Next he offers a literary analysis with particular attention to the text's rhetorical devices, genre, structure, and message. He describes the rhetorical artistry of the exordium (1:1-4) as surpassing that of any other portion of the New Testament. He regards it as conveying the author's basic mode of argumentation about Christ and the new order of salvation: "the new *corresponds* to the old, but *surpasses* it, and does so absolutely, by providing the *perfection* of the true, spiritual order" (p. 36).

The bulk of Attridge's volume is devoted to a verse-by-verse exposition of the individual passages. In the main text of the commentary he treats the words and images, the literary patterns or forms, the major biblical sources, and the ancient parallels. Below the main text there are many footnotes (one for almost every sentence in many places!) that refer to other translations, offer the full texts of or references to more ancient parallels (especially Philo and Qumran), and direct readers to relevant books and articles by modern scholars.

The focus of the volumes in the Hermeneia commentary series is the historical setting of the text in the context of ancient history, religion, and culture. According to its stated editorial policy printed at the beginning of each volume, "the series eschews for itself homiletical translation of the Bible." However, Attridge does treat Hebrews as a theological text and does take seriously its religious content. Readers may glean many theological insights from Attridge's commentary, but they will need to do the work of extracting them for themselves for the most part.

William L. Lane's two volume *Hebrews 1—8* and *Hebrews 9—13* (1991) appears in the Word Biblical Commentary, a series that describes its contributors as "evangelical" in the term's "positive, historic sense of a commitment to Scripture as divine revelation, and to the truth and power of the Christian gospel" (p. x). In his preface, Lane describes Hebrews as confronting ultimate questions about life and death in an attempt "to breathe new life into men and women who suffer a failure of nerve because they live in an insecure, anxiety-provoking society" (p. xii).

While admitting that the limits of historical knowledge preclude a positive identification of the author, Lane describes the author as a skilled rhetorician, well educated by Hellenistic standards, intensely religious, a pastoral theologian, having an "architectural mind." After weighing the data and various proposals about the origin of Hebrews, he concludes that Hebrews is best viewed as a sermon or homily intended to be read aloud in a Christian house church at Rome in the late 60s of the first century CE.

Lane divides the text of Hebrews into five major sections: the revelation of God through his Son (1:1—2:18), the high priestly character of the Son (3:1—5:10), the high priestly office of the Son (5:11—10:39), loyalty to God through persevering faith (11:1—12:13), and orientation for life as Christians in a hostile world (12:14—13:25). He defines the purpose of Hebrews in this way: "to strengthen, encourage, and exhort the tired and weary members of a house church to respond with courage and vitality to the prospect of a renewed suffering in view of the gifts and resources God has lavished upon them" (p. c).

The major traditions that shaped the author's thought, according to Lane, were the Greek Bible, Hellenistic Judaism, apocalyptic Judaism, and (especially) the Hellenistic wing of early Christianity (as seen in Acts 7 and Paul's letters). The author viewed the Old Testament as a valid and significant witness to God's redemptive word and deed not only in the past but also (and especially) in the present. While the pastoral dimension was most important to the author, his synthetic high Christology focused on Jesus as the incarnate Son of God contributed to the acceptance of his work into the Christian canon of Holy Scripture.

The exposition of the individual passages follows the format of the Word Biblical Commentary series. Lane gives to Hebrews 1:1–4 the title "God Has Spoken the Ultimate Word in His Son," which he regards as the central theme of the whole work. He presents an extensive bibliography of earlier studies, a new translation ("In the past God spoke at various times and in many ways through the prophets," 1:1), notes on the Greek text, a detailed literary analysis ("Form/Structure/Setting"), a verse-by-verse exposition ("Comment"), and final observations ("Explanation"). Lane observes that in 1:1–4 the author gave christological precision to a cluster of ideas derived from Hellenistic Judaism and showed his skill as a creative theologian who brought together wisdom and priestly motifs in a tightly formulated statement concerning the dignity and achievement of Jesus the Son of God.

The most comprehensive and up-to-date entry point to the study of Hebrews appears in **Craig R. Koester**'s Introduction to (pp. 17–131) and Bibliography in (pp. 133–168) his Anchor Bible volume *Hebrews* (2001). The Anchor Bible commentary series seeks to make accessible to the modern reader all the significant historical and linguistic knowledge that bears on the interpretation of the biblical record. It is not sponsored by any ecclesiastical organization and is not intended to reflect any particular theological doctrine.

A summary of Koester's positions in the Introduction provides a roadmap or framework for locating the many studies of Hebrews treated in this survey of recent scholarship. In sketching the history of the interpretation and influence of Hebrews, Koester distinguishes three key moments: the place of Hebrews in the theological and christological controversies in the fourth and fifth centuries, its role in the debates between Catholics and Protestants about priesthood and sacrifice in the sixteenth century, and its emergence within historical criticism in the nineteenth and twentieth centuries (and the controversies about its authorship, context of composition, and place in the history of Christianity and history of religion).

In treating the social setting of Hebrews, Koester first distinguishes three phases in the history of the Christian community addressed in the work: proclamation and conversion, persecution and solidarity, and friction and malaise. He observes that the author of Hebrews sought to reinvigorate community life by reaffirming and developing the confession of faith and by calling listeners to actions that would contribute to the community's well-being. While focusing on the symbolic resources of Judaism, the author also appropriated and transformed images from Greco-Roman culture in ways that supported a distinctively Christian confession.

Whether or not Hebrews should be called a sermon, Koester observes that it was certainly written to be read aloud, and that it incorporates elements of epideictic rhetoric (since it maintains the values that listeners hold) and deliberative rhetoric (since it seeks to dissuade them from apostasy and move them toward a clearer faith commitment). He interprets Hebrews according to an outline well known in ancient Greek and Latin oratory: exordium (1:1–2:4), proposition (2:5–9), arguments (2:10–12:27), peroration (12:28–13:21), and epistolary prescript (13:22–25). In the "arguments" section he discerns three series, each consisting of an argument (2:10 – 5:10; 7:1 – 10:25; 11:1 – 12:24) and a transitional digression (5:11 – 6:20; 10:26–39; 12:25–27). In summoning the listeners to a renewed commitment to God, Christ, and the Christian community, the author of Hebrews develops a logical and intellectually persuasive argument, speaks from the heart and plays on the emotions, and communicates with the help of many images and various figures of speech.

Hebrews is first and foremost a work of theology. In matters of cosmology and eschatology the author operates in both spatial and temporal terms and with an eye toward both the present and the future. In treating Christ, the author emphasizes his preexistence and constancy, the importance of the earthly Jesus, and the priesthood and exaltation of Christ. While the promises made to Abraham establish the goal of God's design, the Sinai covenant (the Law) provided only limited means for dealing with sin, whereas the new covenant through the death of Christ provided the definitive means of atonement for sin so that people might come to a full and final relationship with God.

According to Koester, in developing his theological argument, the author interprets Christ in light of the Old Testament and the Old Testament in light of Christ. He construes the actions of God and Christ in categories taken from the Levitical cult: purification, sanctification, and atonement. And he speaks about the outcome of God's designs through Christ's redemptive suffering in terms of completion or perfection. The proper human response is faith in its twofold sense of receiving the message of the gospel and of persevering in the Christian confession. Koester concludes that since there are no clear allusions to the Lord's Supper in Hebrews, we ought not to presuppose the Lord's Supper as a background against which to interpret Hebrews.

An especially valuable feature of Koester's volume is his extensive 34-page Bibliography on Hebrews. It not only covers commentaries from 1750 onward and modern scholarly books and articles, but it also provides information about earlier commentaries (divided into three periods — from 100 to 600, from 600 to 1500, and from 1500 to 1750 CE) and where to find them.

In the Commentary proper (pp. 169–584) Koester treats Hebrews 1:1–4 as part of the "exordium," which for him extends to 2:4. To 1:1–4 he gives the title "God Spoke by a Son." For each passage he provides a fresh translation: "God, having spoken on many occasions and in many forms to the forebears of old by the prophets" (1:1). In his extensive Notes (on nearly every word and phrase), he offers philological observations and calls attention to biblical sources as well as to parallels in Philo's works and in other early Jewish and Christian texts.

In the section labeled "Comment," Koester offers a brief literary analysis and divides his exposition of 1:1–4 into two parts: God has spoken (1:1–2) and the exalted Son (1:3–4). Here Koester attends not only to the rich theological content of the text but also to its literary function within Hebrews as a whole. By means of these "comments," Koester seeks to give what he describes as "a sustained reading of Hebrews" in a nontechnical style and deals with the "major interpretive and theological questions." His hope is that those who are drawn to Hebrews because of its subject matter — God, Christ, and the life of faith — will also find help in reflecting on the meaning of Hebrews for Christian life today.

The Actualization of Hebrews

The editors of the Interpretation series ("A Bible Commentary for Teaching and Preaching") made a wise decision when they assigned their volume on *Hebrews* (1997) to **Thomas G. Long**, then professor of preaching and worship at Princeton Theological Seminary. While making use of the best technical commentaries on Hebrews, Long brings to the text the concerns and sensitivities of an experienced teacher and preacher. By his insights into Hebrews as a sermon, Long opens up the biblical text, makes connections with life today, and illustrates how this biblical sermon can be actualized. In particular, he highlights how the author of Hebrews dealt with the pastoral problem of spiritual weariness by focusing on the person of Jesus Christ.

Drawing on textual evidence in Hebrews and on the common opinion of modern scholars, Long describes the community addressed in the text as in large part suffering from spiritual exhaustion: "tired of serving the world, tired of worship, tired of Christian education, tired of being peculiar and whispered about in society, tired of the spiritual struggle, tired of trying to keep their prayer life going, tired even of Jesus" (p. 3). Church attendance was down, and many persons seemed to be considering leaving the community and falling away from the Christian faith.

What is most remarkable, according to Long, is the preacher's conviction that this state of spiritual weariness is best met by Christology and preaching. His solution was not improved group dynamics, conflict management techniques, or more lively liturgies (however valuable these may be!). Rather, the author of Hebrews wrote a long and complicated exposition of the theological significance of Jesus' death and resurrection. Faced with the problem of spiritual exhaustion, he was bold enough, even brash enough, to preach to this congregation "in complex theological terms about the nature and meaning of Jesus Christ" (p. 5).

Long's great knowledge of preaching and his extensive experience at it enable him to catch the rhetorical dynamic of Hebrews. Whereas in the hands of biblical specialists, Hebrews can sometimes come off as a dense and even dull theological treatise, Long is always in tune with its oratorical spirit and makes the text come alive. He is sensitive to the various homiletical devices on display and helps today's readers to become aware of them.

For example, in the stern warning presented in Hebrews 5:11—6:12, Long shows how the author moves as "a crafty preacher." The preacher first entices his congregation with the suggestion that the material he is about to present in chapters 7—10 may be too advanced for them, then warns them that there is no turning back for them, and finally encourages them to move forward to greater spiritual maturity. Likewise, in the catalogue of the heroes of faith in Hebrews 11:1 — 12:2, Long explains the rhetorical flow of the passage in terms of the homiletical strategy used by African American preachers: "Start low, go slow, reach higher, strike fire, sit down in a storm." Finally Long shows how Hebrews 12:29 ("for indeed our God is a consuming fire") functions as a dramatic ending to the sermon and how most of chapter 13 consists of announcements (13:1–19) and a closing benediction (13:20–21), which also serves as a reprise of major themes in the body of the sermon.

Besides explaining how Hebrews works as a sermon, Long also demonstrates how "the parabola of salvation"—the glorious Son in heaven, the suffering Son on earth, and the triumphant Son in heaven—runs through the sermon as a whole. He also greatly illumines the central section—Hebrews 7 — 10—by noting how at each point the dynamic of "old" and "new" is developed. And he enlivens his exposition by using examples from life today and by sometimes delivering the exegesis in a homiletic style. Readers can learn much about Hebrews as a sermon and much about effective preaching then and now from Long's commentary.

Fred B. Craddock is another interpreter who is equally sensitive to both the homiletical character of Hebrews and the ways of actualizing the text today in preaching and teaching. Craddock served for many years as professor of preaching and New Testament at Candler School of Theology, Emory University, in Atlanta. He is a respected New Testament exegete and a famous preacher, and so he was the perfect candidate to write what is a book-length treatment of Hebrews for *The New Interpreter's Bible,* Volume 12, pp. 1–173 (1998).

After reflecting on some reasons for the church's relative neglect of Hebrews (its place near the end of the canon, its traditional title, the strange and often difficult idiom in which it is written, the stern nature of its imperatives), Craddock emphasizes the need for patience in reading and studying Hebrews. He suggests: "Be in no hurry to collapse the distance between the church and the text. Restrain the appetite for immediacy, for a 'lesson for today.' Trust that that will come in due season" (p. 6).

Craddock describes Hebrews as not only the most extended treatment of the Old Testament in the New but also (along with Luke) the most respectful of continuity. Rather than calling Hebrews a homily or a sermon, he prefers to describe it as "a sermon containing sermons" (1:5—2:4; 2:5—3:1; 8:1—10:25) after the pattern of the book of Deuteronomy and as interweaving large sections of exposition (1:1–14; 2:5—3:6; etc.) and exhortation (2:1–4; 3:7—4:16; etc.).

Following the format of the twelve-volume *New Interpreter's Bible,* Craddock provides for each pericope in Hebrews of the New International Version and the New Revised Standard Version translations, a literary-rhetorical analysis and a verse-by-verse commentary, and "Reflections." In the commentary proper, he presents in a clear and concise form the essential literary, historical, and theological information needed to understand the text of Hebrews. This feature of Craddock's work will be very helpful for most preachers, teachers, and students.

Where Craddock's work stands out is in the literary-rhetorical analyses and the "Reflections." For example, in treating Hebrews 1:1–4, Craddock points out the various literary-rhetorical techniques used in that text: alliteration (five words in 1:1 beginning with p in Greek), contrast (long ago/in these last days; to our ancestors/to us; by the prophets/by a Son), repetition (of relative pronouns and participles), and temporal sequence (pre-existence, incarnation, and exaltation). He also shows how the prologue creates an atmosphere of trust between the author and his audience, and introduces many of the major themes and texts (Pss 2 and 110) that are prominent in the body of the work.

In the "Reflections" Craddock calls attention to themes that could be developed in prayer, Bible studies, and preaching. With regard to Hebrews 1:1–4, he points to four such topics: God as the primary subject of Christian faith, God's speaking and self-revelation as the cornerstone of Judaism and Christianity, the continuity and discontinuity between Christianity and Judaism, and the artistry and sophistication of early Christians such as the author of Hebrews.

For those in search of further help in the process of actualization, **George H. Guthrie**'s *Hebrews* (1998) in the "NIV Application Commentary" series is another valuable resource. Guthrie has written an important monograph on the literary structure of Hebrews (see pp. 33–35), and has worked on Hebrews in terms of exegesis and pastoral practice for many years. The series is based on the New International Version (NIV), an excellent translation by evangelical biblical scholars. And the contributors and the publisher identify themselves as evangelical Protestants.

The goal of the NIV Application Commentary is to help pastors, teachers, and all kinds of Bible readers with "the difficult but vital task of bringing an ancient message into a modern context." The series is especially designed to guide the reader through the process of moving from the original meaning of a passage to its contemporary significance.

While acknowledging the uncertainty that prevails regarding the introductory issues, Guthrie contends that Hebrews is most plausibly interpreted as a sermon written by a learned Jewish Christian for oral presentation to a house church at Rome in the mid-60s of the first century. This sermon freely interweaves biblical exposition and exhortation, with the goal of encouraging and challenging a faltering community in need of strengthening their commitment by drawing near to God.

What is distinctive about Guthrie's commentary flows from the format of the NIV Application Commentary. Every pericope is treated in three sections. The first section ("Original Meaning") helps the reader understand the text in its original first-century context, with all the usual methods of biblical exegesis. The second section ("Bridging Contexts") helps the reader to discern what is timeless in the timely pages of the New Testament — and what is not. The third section ("Contemporary Significance") allows the biblical message to speak with as much power today as when it was first written.

So, for example, when treating Hebrews 1:1–4, Guthrie presents the New International Version of the text and offers an exegesis ("Original Meaning") under two subheadings: the climax of divine communication (1:1–2a) and the person, work, and status of the Son (1:2b–4). His explication is well informed, clearly stated, and accessible to nonspecialists. Then under "Bridging Contexts," he considers the author's central concerns in 1:1–4 (God, Christ, the word, the church) and focuses on the christological significance of the passage. Finally under "Contemporary Significance" he suggests what themes or ideas in the text might be especially meaningful to people today in preaching and Christian life.

The large amount of space devoted to theological significance and to actualization makes Guthrie's commentary on Hebrews especially helpful for readers today. The ethos of this volume is late twentieth-century Protestant evangelicalism in the United States. It abounds in personal examples, references to other biblical texts and to theological treatises, citations of other literary and cultural resources (especially the writings of C. S. Lewis), and suggestions for preachers and teachers. However, Christians from other traditions can find much in Guthrie's work to enrich their appreciation and actualization of the text.

Evaluation

Readers of Hebrews have been well served in recent years. While there are many good presentations of Hebrews for the general public, the introductory exposition by Donald Hagner is especially well done, coming from a veteran teacher and skilled commentator who can write effectively for a nonspecialist audience.

The three full-scale commentaries by Harold Attridge, William Lane, and Craig Koester are among the best volumes in their respective series. They present comprehensive and balanced introductions, as well as solid expositions of individual passages that reflect the best scholarship on the literary, historical, and theological dimensions of their texts. All three are knowledgeable about where the most pertinent ancient parallels are to be found, conversant with developments in modern research, and sensitive to religious and theological concerns. If budding New Testament scholars want to learn how to study a text and to write a good scholarly commentary, these three books provide good models.

If there is a consensus about anything regarding Hebrews, it is that it is best understood as a sermon in written form. The three midrange commentaries intended for a nonspecialist readership by Thomas Long, Fred Craddock, and George Guthrie mark one of the most interesting and positive developments on Hebrews in recent years. The authors are competent in both biblical studies and homiletics, and so there is a close fit between them and the author of Hebrews. They are well attuned to the author's homiletical techniques and concerns, and so they are able to offer fresh and stimulating readings of specific passages. They not only illustrate the process of actualizing Hebrews today but also greatly illumine the text in its first-century setting.

2
The Mysteries of Hebrews

"Without father, without mother, without genealogy…"
(Heb 7:3a)

In modern scholarship on Hebrews, there is little consensus about the work's exact date and place of origin or about the identity of its author. Most agree that it was written sometime between 60 and 100 CE and has some connection with Italy (see 13:24). Nearly everyone quotes Origen's remark about the authorship: "Who wrote Hebrews, God alone knows." Beyond these very general points there is not much agreement.

The relative disregard that Hebrews suffered from historical critics in the nineteenth and twentieth centuries was due in large part to their inability to place it securely in the history and geography of first-century Judaism and early Christianity. The author's own description of the mysterious Melchizedek cited above has often been invoked to describe the mysteries or riddles surrounding its author, date, place of composition, community addressed in it, historical and intellectual background, religious and sociological setting, literary features, and so forth. While recent scholarship has not definitively solved these mysteries, some good progress has been made largely through the application of "new" social-science and literary-critical methods to this ancient text.

Historical and Intellectual Backgrounds

Hebrews has often been compared with and read in light of the writings of Philo of Alexandria. In *The Intermediary World and Patterns of Perfection in Philo and Hebrews* (1975), **Lala Kalyan Kumar Dey** argues that the sequence of comparisons of Jesus as "Son" with the angels, Moses, Aaron and Levi, and Melchizedek belong to the religious thought world of Hellenistic Judaism represented best by Philo. Dey first describes the character of the intermediary world in Philo and the patterns of religious perfection as the general background for understanding Hebrews. Then he interprets major themes in Hebrews in terms of this general background and of the specific exegetical traditions used by the author in his argument.

In this thought world, angels, the Logos, wisdom, and the like constitute an intermediary world between God and humankind. As intermediaries they are agencies of creation and revelation. This intermediary world mediates an inferior revelation and a religious status of a secondary order. The higher level or "perfection" is characterized by unmediated and direct access to God and by participation in God's primary gifts. The supreme exemplars of the higher level were Moses, who communicated with God face to face; Aaron, who as high priest divests himself of the robe (the universe) and enters the holy of holies (the upper limits of heaven where God dwells); and Isaac, who typified self-learned and self-taught wisdom, as did Melchizedek.

Dey contends that the Christians addressed in Hebrews were not in danger of a relapse into Judaism or suffering "post-apostolic fatigue" but rather were confused and disturbed by the Jewish tradition about perfection and immediacy to God without intervening mediators and about the highest religious status like that of Aaron and Moses. The author of Hebrews, according to Dey, wanted to show that what this Jewish tradition promised was already accessible to his Christian readers through Christ the great high priest who offered himself as the one effective sacrifice for sins and who now enjoys full access to God as the Son of God. And so he set out to demonstrate the superiority of Jesus the Son of God to the angels (1:1 — 2:4), to Moses (3:1–6), and to Levi and Aaron as well as Melchizedek (7:1–28), respectively.

In developing his argument for the superiority of Jesus, the author of Hebrews modified the Jewish tradition by bringing into prominence the incarnation and death of Jesus. Dey states the author's thesis in this way: "Jesus has entered and participated in the realm of imperfection (flesh, blood and temptation) and has accomplished perfection within this realm and thereby has opened the way for others to participate in perfection within this realm of creation and not outside it" (p. 219). In the thought world of Philo and of Hebrews, perfection consists in proximity and access to God, and Jesus has accomplished this perfection for himself. In the author's reinterpretation of the tradition, Christians on earth can now participate in the perfection of Christ and connect with God in heaven through their faith and hope in Christ.

In *The Beginnings of Christian Philosophy: The Epistle to the Hebrews* (1982), **James W. Thompson** situates the author in an Alexandrian Jewish tradition of biblical exegesis that worked within the framework of Greek philosophy before and after Philo. Thompson finds the unity of Hebrews in its dualistic reading of the Old Testament and its emphasis on the transcendence of the Christian possession. The "great salvation" (2:3) has a metaphysical superiority to the word delivered by the angels. Whereas the prior (old covenant) revelation dealt only with the sphere of the tangible (12:18), the worldly (9:1), and the "hand-made" (9:11), Christian experience includes sharing in the heavenly call (3:1), access to God's heavenly sanctuary (10:19–22), and access to the unseen world (11:13). Thompson contends that the theological sections in Hebrews were intended not to combat a specific heresy but rather to demonstrate the greatness of Christian faith in metaphysical terms.

According to Thompson, the best comparative material for studying Hebrews remains the writings of Philo of Alexandria, not because the author of Hebrews read them, but because the two writers represent a tradition of appropriating Platonic elements into biblical exegesis. While stopping short of calling the author a philosopher, Thompson suggests that he had received a secondary education that included instruction in philosophy. What distinguishes Hebrews from other early Christian literature is its use of a common metaphysic that was commonly known in educated circles. In this sense, Hebrews constitutes a transition to Christian philosophy. Nevertheless, its use of metaphysical arguments does not diminish the claim that the drama of Jesus' incarnation and crucifixion is the turn of the ages, allowing a new participation in the "powers of the age to come" (6:4–6).

This approach to Hebrews and its author is based on series of essays in which Thompson analyzes key texts. (Here they are discussed according to the order of the texts in Hebrews rather than according to the order of the chapters in his book.) The point of the catena of biblical texts in Hebrews 1:5–13 is to distinguish between the place of Christ in the heavenly world (1:3) and the place of the angels within the intermediate world. The exalted Christ now abides forever the same (1:8, 11, 12). In Hebrews 3:7—4:11 the goal of the midrash on Psalm 95 and Genesis 2:2 is to give the readers a basis for holding fast to their stable position and so to find true rest *(katapausis)* in the transcendental world at God's side in the abiding and unshakable kingdom.

In Hebrews 5:11–14, the distinction between "basic elements" and mature teachings presupposes the Greek educational distinction between lower and higher studies. In Hebrews, the higher studies concern the heavenly high priesthood of Christ that is explained in Hebrews 7. There the dualistic reading of the Old Testament, the use of Hellenistic terminology in 7:3 ("without father, without mother…"), and the focus on the abiding of Christ the exalted one have their closest analogies in Philo's works. In Hebrews 8—10, the treatment of sacrifice reflects metaphysical assumptions that a material sacrifice is inadequate for a true sacrifice, that genuine cleansing cannot be effected by the blood of

animals, and that we must approach God with purity of conscience (understood as the heavenly aspect of human existence).

In Hebrews 11, the celebration of the great heroes of faith is
based on the dualistic distinction between the phenomenal and
invisible worlds, which in turn grounds the definition of faith in
11:1 as "invisible, transcendent reality" *(hypostasis)* and as
"proof" *(elenchos)* and realization of the metaphysically superior
and stable reality represented by God's "unshakable kingdom"
(12:28). In Hebrews 12:18–29, the Jewish eschatological sce-
nario has been reshaped by the author's Platonic metaphysical
dualism that leads him to distinguish between Mount Sinai as
"something that can be touched" (12:18) and Mount Zion as "a
kingdom that cannot be shaken" (12:28). And at the heart of the
closing exhortation in Hebrews 13:9–14 is the fundamental dualism between the sphere of the "flesh" exemplified by "food" and
the heavenly sphere of the Christian altar (13:9–10), between the
"no lasting city" and "the city that is to come" (13:14).

Two prominent mysteries regarding Hebrews concern
whether it should be read against any particular non-Christian
background and where it fits with regard to other early Christian
writings. In *The Epistle to the Hebrews: Its Background of
Thought* (1990), **L. D. Hurst** explores in detail its alleged non-
Christian background(s) and its place in the early Christianity.
What emerges from Hurst's careful analyses is the recognition
that the Old Testament and its developments in Jewish apocalyp-
ticism constitute the most important "background" for reading
Hebrews, and that Hebrews is not entirely an "odd block" in the
New Testament or in early Christianity but rather has strong ties
with writings that are generally regarded as near the center or core
of New Testament theology.

Hurst's critical survey of various non-Christian backgrounds is generally negative in its results. Neither Philo's writings, nor Platonism, nor the Qumran scrolls, nor gnosticism, nor
Samaritanism, nor Jewish Merkabah mysticism can be said to
explain adequately the genesis of the language and thought in

Hebrews. In some sense, however, every one of these proposed "backgrounds" does serve to illumine passages in Hebrews. But just as in Euclidean geometry parallel lines never meet, so in literary analysis the presence of parallels does not establish direct influence or contact. With respect to Hebrews, according to Hurst, what these parallels show is the attempt to apply the teaching of the Old Testament to different and changing circumstances. Instead of proving interdependence, what the parallels reveal is the centrality of the Old Testament and developments of it in the Jewish apocalyptic tradition.

Hurst's critical survey of New Testament writings is more positive in its results. He argues that there are genuine links between Hebrews on the one hand, and Acts 7, Paul's letters, and 1 Peter on the other hand. These links are more in the nature of real "contacts" than mere parallels, though he stops short of arguing for direct influence or use in any case.

In Stephen's speech according to Acts 7, Hurst discerns links with Hebrews in several themes: attitudes toward Jewish worship and the Torah, the divine call to "go out," the people's wandering or homelessness, the word of God as "living," the search for "rest" in relation to Joshua, angels as ordainers of God's Law, and the citation of Exodus 25:40. With regard to Paul's writings, Hurst discovers links in three areas: the destiny of humankind in connection with Christ in the light of Psalm 8; the humbling of Christ as a human, including his obedience and subsequent exaltation; and the role of faith (in Christ, as hope in God's promises, in what is not yet seen, as steadfastness, and as trust in God). While there are many contacts between Hebrews and 1 Peter, Hurst explains them as due mainly to common Greek idioms, independent use of the Old Testament, common Christian tradition, or Pauline influence. However, he regards these similarities as important insofar as the two writings try to bolster faith in the face of persecution, and both are linked to Paul and the Pauline tradition.

Religious and Sociological Settings

According to Hebrews 12:2, Jesus "endured a cross, disregarding its shame." The world in which Hebrews was written regarded honor as a very important value and shame as something to be avoided at all costs. A person was important insofar as he or she was (or was not) honored and admired by others. In *Despising Shame: Honor Discourse and Community Maintenance in the Epistle to the Hebrews* (1995), **David A. deSilva** investigates how the author of Hebrews constructed an alternate arena of honor and dishonor in order to allow the addressees to pursue honor and secure a sense of themselves as honorable by continuing in their Christian commitments, and to inspire in them a fear of dishonoring Christ and his Father by seeking to get approval from the transitory "court of reputation" of this world.

As background for understanding how Hebrews treats honor and shame, deSilva first shows that honor and shame were prominent values for the Greco-Roman world of the first century. His analysis of rhetorical tractates, literary speeches, and ethical treatises illustrates that appeals to attain or preserve honor and avoid shame were expected to persuade people to think or act in certain ways. In this context deSilva characterizes Hebrews as "a deliberative speech which makes extensive use of epideictic rhetoric" (p. 78).

However, within Greco-Roman society (and especially in Hebrews) there was also a lively debate about from where honor should come and whose opinion counts. For philosophers like Aristotle, Seneca, and Epictetus real honor comes from fidelity to philosophical truth and not from popular opinion. For Jews like the authors of Sirach, Wisdom, and 4 Maccabees, honor comes from the pursuit of wisdom, fear of the Lord, and the Torah. The point is that minority cultures developed alternate arenas for fulfilling their members' desire for honor, and that their members had concern for the opinion of a higher court—whether it be nature, the governing principle, Zeus, or the God of Israel. In turn, commitment to the values of the minority group (faith) carried with it the promise of greater honor than the dominant culture could offer.

In highlighting the role of honor and shame in Hebrews, deSilva first explores how the author developed counter-definitions of the honorable and the disgraceful. For the author of Hebrews, faith involves a disregard for one's estimation in society's eyes (the usual understanding of honor) and an exclusive concern for one's honor in the eyes of God. He reminds the addressees that they too had been "publicly exposed to abuse and persecution" (10:33), that Christ himself went to the cross "disregarding its shame" (12:2), and that great heroes of faith like Abraham and Moses also despised shame as most people in their time defined it. By shifting the locus of honor from popular opinion to God, the author encouraged solidarity with Jesus and the replication of his faith.

Next deSilva notes the author's effort at reminding the readers about the supreme honor of Jesus Christ as the Son of God who ranks higher than the angels, or Moses, or the Levitical high priest. Christ is the mediator (see 8:6; 9:15; 12:24) or broker who secures favor from God on behalf of those who have committed themselves to Jesus as client dependents. By giving access to God, Christ affords Christians access to resources for endurance in faith so that they may receive the benefactions promised for the future, to be awarded before God's court at the end of the age. The references to the wilderness generation (3:7—4:13) and Esau (12:16–17) as well as the many warnings sprinkled throughout Hebrews serve as reminders to the addressees to show to God the honor due such a great benefactor and to maintain their loyalty toward Christ who gained for them access to God.

One of the purposes of Hebrews, according to deSilva, is to convince the addressees to disregard society's evaluation of what is honorable and disgraceful and also the society's evaluation of their honor, so that they will be free to persevere in their dedication to the Christian minority culture's distinctive goals, values, and commitments. If they fail to persevere, they will incur the wrath of God and strike a blow against their own honor and dignity. For them the real "court of reputation" is constructed by God, Christ, and fellow Christians. Their path to honor involves embracing the community of faith as a counterculture within Greco-Roman society and perseverance in faith, piety, and gratitude. Within the Christian minority culture, honor and shame serve to motivate the pursuit of Christian virtues, to encourage the performance of deeds that demonstrate obedience to Christ, and to deter the wavering from falling away from their place in God's favor. In *Perseverance in Gratitude: A Socio-Rhetorical Commentary on the Epistle "to the Hebrews"* (2000), deSilva presents a reading of the whole text of Hebrews, with particular attention to its rhetorical strategy (how its author seeks to persuade his audience to remain committed to the Christian movement) and the social effects of accepting the author's ideology as one's own (what kind of church Hebrews seeks to create).

In *Going Outside the Camp: The Sociological Function of the Levitical Critique in the Epistle to the Hebrews* (2001), **Richard W. Johnson** argues that the critique of the Levitical system in Hebrews (especially in 7:1—10:18) functioned sociologically by supporting the author's implicit advocacy of an ideal society, and that his ideal society was both more open to outsiders and more willing to assimilate fully new members than first-century CE Hellenistic Judaism was. He contends that first-century Hellenistic Judaism was a "strong group, strong grid" society within the larger Greco-Roman world; that the ideal society implicitly advocated by the author of Hebrews was weaker in terms of both group and grid than first-century Judaism was; that the critique of the Levitical system in Hebrews was a component of his coherent "weak group, weak grid" cosmology; and that the critique of the Levitical system was related to the overall purpose of the epistle.

Johnson's sociological analysis is based on the anthropologist Mary Douglas's classification of societies according to two parameters: group (the experience of a bounded social unit) and grid (rules that relate one person to others on an ego-centered basis). According to these categories, first-century Hellenistic Judaism was distinctive for its many "strong group" features: aniconic (no images) monotheism, devotion to and practice of the Torah (including observance of the Sabbath, feasts and fasts, circumcision, food laws and limits on table fellowship, and marriage within the group), the Jerusalem Temple and paying the tax that supported it, the socialization of converts into Jewish life, and maintaining links between Judea and the Diaspora. On the internal level, Hellenistic Jews displayed a "strong grid" identity centered around the Temple and the Torah, and manifesting a clear social stratification (priests, Levites, Israelites, proselytes, captives and slaves, marginal persons).

In contrast to Hellenistic Judaism, Johnson maintains that the ideal society implied in Hebrews represents a "weak group, weak grid" profile, which is defined especially in 7:1 — 10:18 (30% of the whole letter) over against the dominant priestly/Levitical system. Indeed the author's portrayal of Jesus as the truly effective high priest and the perfect sacrifice turns upside down the "strong group, strong grid" structure of Hellenistic Jewish society.

The group that the author of Hebrews envisions as destined for the city promised to the believing community is not nationalistic or hostile to outsiders. Johnson finds some links between Hebrews and the Stephen group glimpsed in Acts 7. Within this group there are few rules and few permanent structures, with the most important relationship being that between Christ as the sanctifier and believers as the sanctified. In this kind of society, sin is mainly interior and ethical, there is little or no stress on rituals, purity is understood in moral rather than cultic terms, and suffering is regarded as a discipline. According to Johnson, by challenging the Levitical system the author of Hebrews challenged the particular symbols of first-century Judaism. He set Christ in place of the Levitical nobility and promoted the entry of outsiders into the community of believers (which he considered as welcoming and incorporating outsiders into the city of God).

Another sociological investigation of Hebrews uses the concept of "legitimation" as a way of exploring the relationship between the work's historical situation and its theology. In *Legitimation in the Letter to the Hebrews: The Construction and Maintenance of a Symbolic Universe* (2002), **Iutisone Salevao** argues that the author of Hebrews sought to make Christian faith subjectively plausible to the members of his community by telling them why things are what they are and why they should act upon this knowledge presented as "right knowledge."

The sociological theory used by Salevao is based on the "sociology of knowledge" developed by Peter Berger and Thomas Luckmann in the 1960s. This approach proceeds on the basic premise of the relationship between thought and the social context out of which knowledge arises, and its primary concern is with this correlation. Legitimation refers to the aggregate of ways in which a social order or social world is explained and justified to members of a group. It involves externalization, objectivation, and internalization. Salevao contends that the theology of Hebrews was intended to "legitimate" or explain, justify, and sanctify the situation of the community of its first readers and to elicit a social response from them.

According to Salevao, Hebrews was written by a well-educated Christian of Jewish origin between 70 and 90 CE to members of a house church in or near Rome who were mainly Jewish Christians contemplating a return (or relapse) to Judaism. The addressees faced external pressure experienced as political persecution, social alienation, and hostility from outsiders. They also experienced internal disunity caused by a theological conflict that had manifested itself in the separation of some members from the rest of the congregation. The immediate threat was that this separation not only involved a break in fellowship but also was liable to develop into abandonment of the Christian faith and a possible large scale relapse back into Judaism. This was the immediate threat.

To respond to this threat, the author of Hebrews provided an explanation and a justification (that is, a legitimation) of the separation of his community from Judaism. As a way of describing the community addressed in Hebrews, Salevao uses the sociological concept of "sect": born out of protest, rejecting the established view of reality, egalitarian, offering love and acceptance to its members, a voluntary group, requiring total commitment, and apocalyptic in orientation. Legitimating Christian faith for such a group involved denunciation, contrast, and reinterpretation of traditions. Part of the author's task was to affirm Christianity's superiority to Judaism. More than just an exhortation, Hebrews was designed to inculcate commitment to the Christian community, reaffirm the distinctive identity through the definition of its boundaries, bolster solidarity or cohesion among the members, and legitimate the reality status of the community.

One of the most famous and puzzling texts in Hebrews appears in 6:4–6: "For it is impossible to restore again to repentance those who have once been enlightened…and then have fallen away" (see also 10:26). Salevao interprets this text as part of the author's "legitimating edifice" and as a warning about the irrevocable consequences of apostasy. For him, conversion, baptism-initiation, and acceptance into the Christian community was final, once for all, and unrepeatable. Since apostasy (in this case returning to Judaism) would reverse and abrogate the effect of the conversion-initiation event, it would therefore be irrevocable. The social function of this doctrine would be to keep potential deviants within the institutionalized definitions of reality and to prevent them from apostasizing. The doctrine of the impossibility of a second repentance fits well with the themes of pilgrimage, purity/holiness, and new covenant.

Salevao describes the situation behind Hebrews as a "power struggle" over the community's relationship to Judaism. And so one of the author's major tasks was to explain the superiority of Christianity and the inferiority of Judaism. To do so, the author used the device of typology to demonstrate the superiority of

Christ vis-à-vis angels, Moses, the Levitical priesthood, the earthly tabernacle, and the old covenant. Likewise, he repeatedly employed terms such as "better," "new," and "perfect" to assert the superiority of Christianity. And he interpreted the Christ-event as the center-point that gave meaning and purpose to the entire history of salvation.

Literary Matters

The literary structure of Hebrews has been a source of fascination among biblical scholars and has produced many learned solutions. Nevertheless, there is still controversy over such fundamental issues as the primary dividing points in the book, the organizational principle around which the author has built his book, and the methodology by which the structure of the book may be discerned.

Perhaps the most persistent, prolific, and influential scholar on Hebrews over the last forty years has been **Albert Vanhoye**, a Jesuit who has taught for many years at the Pontifical Biblical Institute in Rome. The focus of his work has been the literary structure of Hebrews and how it contributes to conveying the book's theological content. Most of his books and articles have been published in French. But a slim volume in English entitled *Structure and Message of the Epistle to the Hebrews* (1989) offers a convenient entry point for English readers who want to know about Vanhoye's approach.

Despite his English title, Vanhoye quickly explains that Hebrews is a sermon (not an epistle) and was written to Christians (not to Hebrews) by someone other than Paul (though with ties to Pauline theology). While admitting that nothing about Jesus' person or life corresponded to the biblical (or pagan) concept of priesthood, Vanhoye suggests that the author of Hebrews was led to explore the unique priesthood of Christ most likely by the early interpretations of Jesus' death as a sacrifice for sins and by the prominence of the priesthood of Aaron in the Old Testament.

The basic thesis of Vanhoye's many publications on Hebrews can be summarized in his own words: "A systematic study of the Greek text of the Epistle to the Hebrews has led me to the conclusion that the author of the Epistle has structured his work with great care and has made use of fixed literary devices to indicate what he has done" (p. 75). He describes the author as having "written his work with a talent without equal, making use of structuralizing techniques which came to him from his Jewish-Hellenistic education" (p. 19).

Vanhoye's starting point for analyzing the literary structure of Hebrews is the presence of five short passages that announce the topic to be discussed next: 1:4; 2:17–18; 5:9–10; 10:36–39; and 12:13. Other rhetorical techniques giving structure to Hebrews are inclusion (using the same words at the beginning and the end of a unit), hook words (beginning a section with words from the end of the preceding section), characteristic terms (repeating words within a section to give it a distinctive shape), alternation of literary genres (changing from one kind of discourse to another), and symmetrical arrangements (forming patterns from correspondences in many details).

With these and other rhetorical devices in mind, Vanhoye discerns a detailed outline of Hebrews and presents on pages 75–109 a structured English translation of the entire text designed to illustrate its movement and the presence of the various techniques with the help of different typefaces and other typographical devices. In addition to the exordium (1:1–4) and the peroration (13:20–21, plus the appendix in 13:22–25), Vanhoye divides the main text into five major parts: 1 — a name so different from the name of the angels (1:5 — 2:18); 2 — Jesus as high priest worthy of faith (3:1 — 4:14) and as compassionate high priest (4:15 — 5:10); 3 — a preliminary exhortation (5:11 — 6:20), Jesus as high priest according to the order of Melchizedek (7:1–28), come to fulfillment (8:1 — 9:28), cause of an eternal salvation

(10:1–18), and final exhortation (10:19–39); 4—the faith of the people of old (11:1–40) and the need for endurance now (12:1–13); and 5—choosing straight ways (12:14—13:19). Moreover, Vanhoye regards the five main units as arranged concentrically (A–B–C–B–A) around 9:1–10 and 9:11–14 in general and around the name of Christ in the beginning of 9:11 ("Christ, he…") in particular.

In response to early Christians asking about priesthood, the author of Hebrews, says Vanhoye, replied: "Christ is our priest." But rather than applying to the mystery of Christ the idea of priesthood as it had been understood in Jewish and pagan circles, he deepened its meaning to the point of completely renewing it. He argued that Christ not only possesses priesthood but also that he is the one and only priest in the full sense of the word (as one who mediates access to God). According to Hebrews, Christ is the only one to have opened to men and women the way that leads to God and that unites them among themselves.

In *The Rhetorical Composition and Function of Hebrews 11 In Light of Example Lists in Antiquity* (1988), **Michael R. Cosby** argues that the passage plays a vital role in the author's overall attempt to instill in his discouraged audience a tenacious faith that will triumphantly face the present difficult circumstances. He also insists that the author wrote his sermon to make an impact on the ears of his audience and to sound persuasive, and so Cosby wants to show how listening to the Greek text opens up new horizons of understanding and appreciation.

As comparative material Cosby uses lists of examples from ancient literature. He observes that while the use of examples is a common rhetorical device in antiquity, there are not enough lists of examples to warrant speaking about example lists as a literary genre. Nevertheless, he is convinced that one can learn much about Hebrews 11 from the relatively few cases that do exist.

Hebrews 11 starts with the functional (rather than formal) definition of faith. The opening verse (11:1) relies on various sound techniques in Greek to get the reader's attention. In this

context "faith" means firm confidence in the things we hope for
as well as the proof of the things we cannot see. In 11:3–31, the
author of Hebrews makes abundant use (eighteen times!) of the
rhetorical device of anaphora; that is, beginning each unit with
the same word or phrase ("By faith"). The effect is to make the
large number of examples seem to be representative of an even
larger number that could be cited. Moreover, by giving several
examples of the faith shown by Abraham and Moses, the author
attaches special prominence to these characters. In 11:32–40 the
author of Hebrews shifts rhetorical gears and uses different
rhetorical techniques such as asyndeton (omitting conjunctions)
and polysyndeton (multiplying conjunctions), as well as isocolon
(clauses of equivalent length). Throughout Hebrews 11, the
author uses various secondary literary techniques: antithesis
(placing contrary statements in juxtaposition), hyperbole (exag-
geration), paranomasia (wordplays or puns), and circumlocution
(using several words where one would suffice).

By demonstrating the rhetorical techniques in Hebrews 11
and their desired effect on those who heard them and by compar-
ing these techniques with those employed in other ancient example lists, Cosby succeeds in uncovering valuable insights into the
rhetorical form and function of the catalogue of the heroes of
faith. He has confirmed in an effective way the oral and rhetorical
character of Hebrews as a sermon.

After surveying past proposals about the structure of
Hebrews and evaluating their approaches, **George H. Guthrie** in
The Structure of Hebrews: A Text-Linguistic Analysis (1994)
moves from detailed examination of individual passages to discerning the relationships among the sections of the author's discourse as a whole. While incorporating the work of earlier
scholars (especially that of Albert Vanhoye), he focuses on the
isolation of individual units by the identification of unit boundaries, sets forth various means of discerning interrelationships
among the units in Hebrews, and clarifies the logic behind the
arrangement and order of those units.

In his "text-linguistic" study of Hebrews, Guthrie's starting point is "cohesion shift" analysis; that is, changes from one pericope to another in genre, topic, spatial and temporal indicators, actor, subject, verb tense, mood, person, number, reference, and lexical items. For example, between the anthology of biblical quotations to prove the Son's superiority to the angels in 1:5–14 and the exhortation to take God's word seriously in 2:1–4 there are shifts in genre, topic, actor, subject, verb person, verb number, and reference fields. In Hebrews as a whole, Guthrie finds twenty-two "high level" cohesion shifts and thirty-three "median level" cohesion shifts.

A second clue to the structure of Hebrews is provided by the author's frequent use of the rhetorical device of *inclusio;* that is, employing the same or similar words to begin and end a unit, and so to mark it as a unit. For example, Hebrews 3:12 and 3:19 open and close the unit with the verb "see" *(blepo)* and the noun "unbelief" *(apistia).* Guthrie finds eighteen cases of inclusio in Hebrews and notes that there are many correspondences between the units identified by cohesion shift analysis and those marked by inclusio.

A third step in Guthrie's text-linguistic analysis concerns lexical items and pronouns used in promoting textual cohesion throughout Hebrews. Some prominent lexical items include the noun *theos* (God) and pronouns referring to God, designations and pronouns referring to Jesus as God's Son, terms semantically related to "the word of God," and pronouns used to refer to members of the Christian community (the author, his hearers, or both). A fourth step involves tracking the techniques employed by the author to effect transitions. These include "hook words" or catchwords, overlapping constituents, parallel introductions, and intermediary transitions.

What emerges from Guthrie's text-linguistic analysis is a detailed outline of Hebrews that highlights its interweaving of expositional sections (explaining biblical texts in light of the Christ event) and hortatory sections (warning and encouraging).

He divides the expositional material into an introduction (1:1–4) and two main movements: the position of the Son in relation to the angels (1:5 — 2:18) and the position of the Son, our high priest, in relation to the earthly sacrificial system (4:14 — 10:25). He categorizes the rest of the material (2:1–4; 3:1 — 4:13; 5:11 — 6:12; 10:26 — 13:19) as exhortation. He locates the center points for the hortatory material in the warning at 6:4–8 ("it is impossible to restore again to repentance…") and for the expositional material in the affirmation at 8:1–2 ("we have such a high priest…"). On the basis of his text–linguistic analysis, Guthrie describes the purpose of Hebrews in this way: "to exhort the hearers to endure in their pursuit of the promised reward, in obedience to the word of God, and especially on the basis of their new covenant relationship with the Son" (p. 143).

Rather than leading readers straight through the text of Hebrews, **Kenneth Schenck** in *Understanding the Book of Hebrews: The Story Behind the Sermon* (2003) uses a variety of literary methods — narrative analysis, structuralism, and rhetorical criticism — to try to get at the assumptions or presuppositions behind the book, not so much on the historical level but especially on the conceptual and theological levels. He describes the thought of Hebrews as fundamentally narrative in orientation; that is, the arguments of Hebrews center on the story of how God has provided salvation to his people through Christ.

Schenck defines "plot" as the combination of settings (the times and places), events (the things that happen), and characters (those who participate in the things that happen). The settings in space include the highest heaven and the created realm, while the settings in time comprise the former age, the last days or "today," and the age to come (forever). The events are spread over the "former age" (from creation to the earthly life of Jesus) and the "age of Christ" (from his death and exaltation to the last judgment). The characters include God, the devil, the angels, Moses, the prophets, the Levitical priests, Christ, the former leaders of the community, and the author and his audience.

The central character is Christ. The problem that he has to overcome is sin, because of which humans experience shame rather than glory and death rather than eternal life. The solution to this problem comes in two stages: (1) Christ defeats the devil's power over death by offering himself as an atoning sacrifice and (2) God removes the created realm and everything in the universe that is "shakable." Not only by the prologue in 1:1–4 but also by the anthology of biblical quotations in 1:5–14, the author of Hebrews establishes from the start his conviction that Christ has replaced the angels as God's new and better mediator to his people. The one who was made lower than the angels when he took human form has been enthroned as the royal Son of God, Christ, and Lord.

Many of the secondary characters in Hebrews function as examples of either faith or disbelief. While the wilderness generation (3:7 — 4:11) and Esau (12:16–17) illustrate the effects of unbelief, the biblical heroes of faith described in chapter 11 show themselves to be exemplars of endurance and faithfulness. In this context Jesus appears as the final and best example of someone in the old age who was faithful to the point of death, even as his death and exaltation inaugurated the new age.

For Christ perfection involves his successful, sinless completion of the human experience and his subsequent attainment of glory as he is exalted to God's right hand. In the thought of Hebrews, Christ's death atoned for all the sins of the world and rendered obsolete the entirety of the Jewish sacrificial system. The theological center of Hebrews (chapters 5 — 10) seeks to demonstrate that Christ is a priest superior to the Levitical priests, that Christ offers a sacrifice superior to the old covenant sacrifices, and that Christ offers this sacrifice in a sanctuary superior to any of the sanctuaries of the Old Testament.

According to Schenck, the most immediate problem confronting the author of Hebrews was his audience's waning confidence in the certainty of the salvation provided by Christ, an attitude exacerbated by persecution or the threat of persecution from outside the community. Schenck suggests that the author of

Hebrews was a well-educated Greek-speaking Jew who addressed a predominantly Gentile Christian audience at Rome early in the reign of Domitian (81–96 CE).

A Woman Author?

A definite exception to the prevailing vagueness about the authorship of Hebrews is **Ruth Hoppin**. She argues that Hebrews was written by an early Christian woman named Priscilla (also known as Prisca) from Rome to Ephesus in 65 CE. In her book *Priscilla's Letter: Finding the Author of the Epistle to the Hebrews* (1997) Hoppin revives, expands, and updates a hypothesis proposed in 1900 by Adolph von Harnack, the most famous German Protestant early church historian and theologian of his time.

On the basis of evidence within the text of Hebrews, Hoppin rejects the traditional idea that Paul wrote Hebrews but suggests that the author did have connections with Paul and Timothy (see 13:23). That the author was a woman is indicated for Hoppin by the author's feminine psychological profile (sympathetic, caring in a parental sense, fastidious, married, etc.) and her tendency to identify with women (shown by the relative prominence of women in Hebrews 11, the so-called catalogue of heroes). By process of elimination it appears that none of the usual male candidates for authorship—Paul, Clement, Barnabas, Apollos, and Aristion—fits the profile.

According to that profile, the author must be of Paul's circle, not an eyewitness of Jesus but the disciple of an apostle (see 2:3) with connections at Rome and a ministry to Hebrew Christians who resided in the city to which the letter was first sent, an expert in Greek, and trained in rhetoric. And also there must be a cogent explanation as to why the author is not named in the text.

Hoppin contends that the person who best fits this profile is the woman known in Acts as Priscilla and in Romans as Prisca, the wife of Aquila. She brought the learned Apollos to a fuller form of Christianity (see Acts 18:26), was converted by the apostle Peter and may have known Philo of Alexandria, came from a noble Roman family (the Acilian Glabriones) and so was probably well educated, learned about the Old Testament from Essenes at Rome and from anthologies of biblical quotations *(testimonia),* was a Roman and lived for a long time at Rome, married the Jewish freedman Aquila, and was part of the Pauline inner circle.

The sentence "those from Italy send you greetings" in 13:24b indicates to Hoppin that Hebrews was composed at Rome and sent to a city outside Italy. By process of elimination—not Jerusalem, Alexandria, Antioch, Corinth, or Rome—she arrives at Ephesus as the most likely city and a Christian community there dominated by former Essenes (like the Jews who gave us the Qumran scrolls) as the most likely audience. Priscilla and Aquila had recently returned to Rome only to be swept into the persecution of Christians under the emperor Nero there. So, Hoppin contends, Hebrews was written in 65 CE as a continuation and extension of Priscilla's pastoral ministry to Christians in Ephesus. And the reason why Hebrews does not contain its author's name is that it was lost "accidentally on purpose" because a woman (Priscilla) was known to be the author.

Hoppin has performed a service in reviving Harnack's theory and bringing to bear upon it new textual and archaeological discoveries. She has not succeeded in convincing many other scholars (neither did Harnack), mainly because she moves from one questionable hypothesis to another and overstates the certitude of her case drastically. But if nothing else, she has illustrated how hard it is to answer some basic questions about Hebrews (Who? When? Where?) and so contributes to our appreciation of the mystery of Hebrews.

Evaluation

Recent scholarship has not solved all the mysteries of Hebrews. But progress has been made in recognizing that no single historical and/or intellectual background (Philo, Qumran, etc.) explains everything, that sociological models help in clarifying the text and the situation behind it, that the "new" literary methods enhance our appreciation of the author's rhetorical skill, and that the author's identity remains a mystery.

In many scholarly circles, the writings of Philo of Alexandria have assumed a prominent place in the exposition of Hebrews. The monographs by Lala Kalyan Kumar Dey and James Thompson with their focus on the Philonic corpus and the Platonizing worldview behind it continue that approach to some extent. While denying that the author necessarily read the works of Philo and admitting that Philo has exercised too much influence in the interpretation of Hebrews, most expositors today still pay a good deal of attention to Philo's writings as a fruitful source of parallels. But of course, in geometry, parallel lines never meet. Hurst's work serves as a healthy reminder about the basic influence of the Old Testament and Jewish apocalyptic on Hebrews and about the theological links between Hebrews and other New Testament writings. Hebrews is primarily the product of early Christian theology. The Jewish and Greco-Roman parallels take second place.

One of the freshest and best developments in the recent study of Hebrews has been the illumination of the text and the community situation behind it by the application of various sociological models: honor and shame (David deSilva), Mary Douglas's group-grid analysis of societies (Richard Johnson), and legitimation theory drawn from Peter Berger and Thomas Luckmann's sociology of knowledge (Iutisone Salevao). These studies help us to understand how Hebrews redefines honor and shame, promotes an open and flexible community life in comparison with the closed and hierarchical lifestyle of much of contemporary Judaism, and how it works at strengthening identity and relationships among community members. While methodological objections (anachronism, reductionism, etc.) can be made against the sociological analysis of New Testament texts, the three examples pertaining to Hebrews succeed rather nicely in illumining the text, placing it within its first-century sociohistorical context, and making it easier for readers today to understand what may have been going on behind the text.

Recent research on Hebrews has been strongly influenced by Albert Vanhoye's ground-breaking analysis of the book's literary structure. Using insights from earlier scholars, Vanhoye showed that Hebrews is an intricately constructed and rhetorically sophisticated document. While nearly everyone acknowledges a debt to Vanhoye's structural analysis, no one accepts it without some modifications. The recent studies devoted to the literary analysis of Hebrews also show the influence of the "new" methods of rhetorical criticism and orality (Michael Cosby), text linguistics (George Guthrie), and narrative analysis and structuralism (Kenneth Schenck). Although none of these studies overturns Vanhoye's analysis and most claim to build upon it, they do give the impression that the literary artistry of this "word of exhortation" (13:22) is not easily reduced to one outline or one ancient rhetorical pattern.

The identity of the author of Hebrews remains a mystery. Ruth Hoppin's case for Priscilla as the author is ingenious and makes for interesting reading—like a detective story. But in the end it is no more convincing than any of the other attempts in the past. Origen was correct. Only God knows who wrote Hebrews.

3
Hebrews and the "Old Testament"

"Indeed, the word of God is living and active, sharper than
any two-edged sword...." (Heb 4:12a)

If Hebrews is a sermon in written form, then the text on
which this sermon is based is the Old Testament—what the author
refers to as "the word of God" in the text cited above. As a good
preacher, the author alternates between exposition of specific biblical texts and applications to the life of his congregation. Like
other early Christian writers in antiquity, the author is interested
not so much in what the text said in its original biblical setting (as
in modern historical criticism) but more in what it might mean in
the light of the paschal mystery—Jesus' life, death, and resurrec-
tion/exaltation. He views everything in the Old Testament
through a christological lens.

The discovery of the Dead Sea scrolls with their many
examples of biblical interpretation has revived interest in the distinctive ways in which Hebrews deals with the Old Testament.
Whereas the Qumran people interpreted their Scriptures in the
light of their movement's history and life, early Christian works
like Hebrews developed a Christ-centered hermeneutic of the Old
Testament. This revived interest is nicely illustrated by several
monographs on the treatment of biblical hermeneutics, biblical
figures, and biblical texts in Hebrews.

Biblical Hermeneutics

In modern times the most common historical explanation for the composition of Hebrews has been the "relapse" theory; that is, the author was trying to prevent Jewish Christians from returning to Judaism and to Jewish rituals. Another theory takes a more philosophical approach in the sense that the author was trying to wean his audience away from materialistic forms of religion, whether Jewish or pagan. In *Hebrews and Hermeneutics: The Epistle to the Hebrews as a New Testament Example of Biblical Interpretation* (1979), **Graham Hughes** proposes a third approach: The author of Hebrews wanted to present a hermeneutical reflection on how Jesus' work represents the end term of his own familiar Jewish institutions. In other words, Hebrews is the first attempt at a Christian biblical theology.

Hughes contends that the author's concept of Jesus as the eschatological high priest arose out of his own theological preoccupations with the relationships between the covenants. Observing that the prologue (1:1–4) is preeminently about the Word in the Son, he first shows how in Hebrews 1—7 Jesus the Word of God is compared with three agents of Old Testament revelation—angels, Moses, and Levitical priests—and is shown to be both in continuity with them and superior to them. Next Hughes explains how in Hebrews the Word of God is a history of promise moving toward the unshakable kingdom (see 12:27), how Jesus as the final form of God's word relates to the earlier words, and how the doctrinal or more theological parts of Hebrews set the two covenants against one another while the hortatory or paraenetic sections stress their continuity.

Then Hughes argues that a knowledge of Jesus' life was theologically indispensable for the portrayal of Jesus as the "pioneer" (the model of faith) and as the "priest" (the means of salvation). Though not strictly demanded by the Old Testament and the kerygmatic traditions about Jesus, the high priestly Christology was not excluded by them and was at least permitted. As pioneer Jesus stood firmly within the history of a people who must look to the future believingly, while as priest he is now the means of their participating already in the eschatological realities.

The author of Hebrews emerges from Hughes's study as a creative theologian who struggled with the historical structures of revelation and the relationship between the old and the new covenants. In other words, the author worked diligently at what we call hermeneutics. Indeed, according to Hughes, the author offers a model for a Christian approach to hermeneutics. This hermeneutical approach proceeds from faith, is self-critical in deciding what biblical interpretations are and are not legitimate, shows respect for tradition(s), addresses unbelief from the perspective of strong belief, and is acutely conscious of the "not yet" and eschatological element of Christian faith. Hughes concludes that Hebrews is "the joyfully confident testimony of a Christian...whose security palpably rests in the things of which he writes to his friends" (p. 135).

The author of Hebrews has sometimes been accused of distorting the meaning of the Jewish Scriptures. **Dale F. Leschert** investigates this charge in *Hermeneutical Foundations of Hebrews: A Study in the Validity of the Epistle's Interpretation of Some Core Citations from the Psalms* (1994). He defines the seriousness of the charge in this way: "If, indeed, it is true that the writer of Hebrews uses inferior methods of interpretation to distort the meaning of the OT, the credibility of his message must also be called into question to the extent that it rests upon a faulty foundation" (p. 4). However, on the basis of several detailed examinations of how certain texts from the Psalms are used in Hebrews, Leschert argues that the author of Hebrews "interprets in a manner consistent with historical-grammatical hermeneutics without distorting the intended meaning of the OT" (p. 16).

Leschert first presents exegetical analyses of how three texts from the Psalms are treated in Hebrews. He first shows how in Hebrews 1:8–9 the author used Psalm 45:6–7 ("Your throne, O God, endures forever and ever....Therefore God, your God, has

anointed you with the oil of gladness beyond your companions")
to support his claim that since here the Father addresses the Son
as "God," so Jesus is superior to the angels. Leschert contends
that the psalm was originally messianic in intent, that the writer
believed that the psalm was fulfilled in Christ as the heir to
David's throne and as God, and that a human king who foreshad-
ows the coming divine Messiah satisfies both the historical setting and the exalted language of the psalm.

Next Leschert shows that the messianic application of Psalm
8:4–6 ("What are human beings that you are mindful of them…?")
to Jesus in Hebrews 2:5–9 reflects the perception that only Jesus
Christ could fulfill the ideals for humankind set forth in the psalm,
and so it found its messianic fulfillment in Jesus. Then he argues
that the application of the concept of rest as both physical and spiritual in Psalm 95:7–11 to the contemporary generation in Hebrews
3:7–4:11 is consistent with Psalm 95 and sensitive to the broader
teaching of the Old Testament on the subject.

The second part of Leschert's work concerns the hermeneutical methods used by the author in incorporating biblical texts
into his argument. After noting the various definitions of
"midrash," he maintains that the author's treatment of Psalm
95:7–11 in Hebrews 3:7–4:11 does not qualify as "midrash" on
the levels of its presuppositions, hermeneutical techniques, or literary features. Moreover, analysis of the author's treatment of
Melchizedek in Hebrews 7 reveals that it cannot be classified as
exegesis or midrash or Philonic allegory. Instead, the most appro-
priate term is "typology" understood as an analogy rooted in a
genuine historical correspondence.

On the basis of these textual probes, Leschert concludes
that in using Old Testament texts the author is consistent with
their intended meaning, faithful to a Septuagintal version, and in
continuity with traditional interpretations. Moreover, according
to Leschert, the author avoided creative methodologies (those
that might distort), used standard expository methods (explanation, illustration-typology, application), and never interpreted in

a manner that is incompatible with historical-grammatical hermeneutics.

Biblical Figures

In Hebrews there are major and direct references to Moses in 3:1–6 and 11:23–27, as well as passing mentions of Moses in 8:5 and 9:19. In *Moses in the Letter to the Hebrews* (1979), **Mary Rose D'Angelo** argues that Moses' theological function in the letter is "to assist in the articulation of the Christology of Christ's relation to God" (p. 13).

Taking as her starting point the examples of faith displayed by Moses according to Hebrews 11:23–27, D'Angelo shows that Moses emerges as an example of endurance. He is Moses the martyr. Moreover, the deeds that Moses performs and the choices that he makes "by faith" are grounded on or motivated by a vision of the unseen (see 11:27). Indeed, by sharing the opprobrium or reproach of Christ (see 11:26), Moses came to be a "saint" conformed by suffering to Christ the savior who originates and perfects his holiness. In short, Moses is a "Christian martyr." The question is, How did Moses become a Christian?

In Hebrews 3:1–6 there is a comparison between Moses who was faithful in God's house as a servant (3:2, 5) and Jesus who is faithful over God's house as a son (3:6). While Numbers 12:7 ("Not so with my servant Moses; he is entrusted with all my house") is the key biblical text here, D'Angelo contends that the passage must be understood also with reference to other texts, chiefly 1 Chronicles 17:14. Moreover, she argues that the appeal to Moses' uniquely intimate vision of God (in comparison with mere prophets) in Numbers 12:7 became the subject of much speculation in later Jewish texts. Likewise, the "house" in which Moses was faithful became identified in these sources variously as the *familia* on high, the whole created world, the tabernacle or temple, and God's people (the house of Israel). These traditions of interpretation suggest that the Moses of Hebrews is a mystic, entrusted above all with God's house by his ascent and vision of God. Thus the Son differs from Moses, as the Son is greater than the angels. And Moses is greater than the angels insofar as Moses caught a glimpse of the Son as the revelation of God's glory: "he persevered as though he saw him who is invisible" (Heb 11:27).

The mentions of Moses in Hebrews 8—9 provide the occasion for D'Angelo to reflect on the soteriological function of the Mosaic Law in Hebrews. Because Moses saw "the seeable of the Unseen," the Law has a real, though limited, dispensational role in the economy of salvation. Moses as the receiver and deliverer of the oracles of God, Moses' institution of the antitypical role of the high priest, and the inauguration of the covenant all explicate the soteriological role of Jesus insofar as they all derive from it.

D'Angelo concludes that the portrayal of Moses in Hebrews is determined primarily by a christological decision on the part of the author. Not only the glory of Moses that is compared to that of Christ in Hebrews 3:1–6, but also Moses' enduring faith praised in 11:23–27 and his ministry of witness in Hebrews 8—9 are the result of his vision of the dead and risen Lord (see 11:27).

Chapter 7 is sometimes regarded as the focus of the entire text of Hebrews, since there the author develops in detail the concept of a priesthood "according to the order of Melchizedek," a theological theme found nowhere else in the New Testament. In *A History of Interpretation of Hebrews 7,1–10 from the Reformation to the Present* (1976), **Bruce Demarest** focuses on how the passages about Melchizedek in Genesis 14:18–20 and Psalm 110:4 become part of the argument in Hebrews 7:1–10. Demarest notes that the christological significance of the text, its acknowledged difficulty, and the variety of interpretations that it has inspired provide sufficient reason for undertaking a history of its exegesis. In this history Demarest seeks both to trace the study of Hebrews in general and of 7:1–10 in particular over the past five hundred years, and to arrive at an exegesis that is as enlightened and responsible as possible.

Hebrews 7:1–10 concerns the excellence of Melchizedek, his person, and his priesthood in relation to the person and priesthood of Christ. After describing the priesthood of Melchizedek in 7:1–3, in 7:4–10 the author argues that Melchizedek is superior to Abraham and to the Levites descended from him in three ways: Melchizedek received tithes from Abraham, bestowed a blessing on Abraham, and "lives on" whereas the Levitical priests have succumbed to death. The thread running through Demarest's history of interpretation is found in Hebrews 7:3: "Without father, without mother, without genealogy, having neither beginning of days nor end of life, but resembling the Son of God, he remains a priest forever." One of the persistent issues in the history of interpretation is whether "without father, without mother" establishes the humanity and divinity of Jesus.

Demarest recounts the history of the interpretation of Hebrews 7:1–10 in five sections: the age of the Reformation, the seventeenth century, the eighteenth century, the nineteenth century, and the twentieth century. The starting point was the Reformation debate over the Catholic tradition according to which the bread and wine given by Melchizedek to Abraham were a type of the sacrifice of the Mass. From Erasmus to the various Protestant Reformers throughout the sixteenth century there was a tendency to focus on the person of Christ instead of the Eucharist and to take the passage as concerned with the nature and duration of the priesthood of Christ. This trend continued into the seventeenth century as there developed a wide range of opinions about the Christology implied in the text as it was interpreted differently among Lutherans, Calvinists, Arminians, and Puritans.

In the eighteenth century the text became the object of attention from Deists and rationalists, as well as from antiquarians, pietists, and "transitional theologians." The nineteenth century saw the rise of "critical" or modern commentaries that offered philological, grammatical, and historical interpretations that sought to uncover the design of the author and the meaning of the text in relation to those to whom it was first directed. It was also the time when

Philo's writings became the most important source of parallels and when attempts were made at an objective description of the theology of Hebrews. The twentieth century saw the quest for the history-of-religions derivation of the leading religious and theological concepts in Hebrews, the mainstreaming of modern Catholic exegesis as represented by Ceslas Spicq and Albert Vanhoye, and the discovery of a text (11QMelchizedek) about a heavenly-eschatological-warrior figure named Melchizedek among the Dead Sea scrolls.

In his own interpretation of Hebrews 7:1–10, Demarest finds Psalm 110:4 ("You are a priest forever according to the order of Melchizedek") more important than the Samaritan, Philonic, and Qumran parallels, and suggests that the author depicted Melchizedek as "without father, without mother, without genealogy" simply because no mention is made in Genesis 14 about Melchizedek's father, mother, or genealogy. He resists the eucharistic interpretation and the tradition that Hebrews 7:3 concerns the humanity and divinity of Jesus. He concludes that the Melchizedek of Genesis 14 serves as a type of Christ in three ways: as a harbinger of Christ as the "king of righteousness" and "king of peace" who unites in his person the priestly and royal prerogatives, as one whose priesthood was based not on genealogical descent but rather on personal worth and divine appointment, and as an earthly figure of the eternal Son of God who in reality possesses neither beginning nor end of personal existence.

Whereas Demarest traced interpretations of Melchizedek in Hebrews 7 over the last five centuries, **Fred L. Horton** in *The Melchizedek Tradition: A Critical Examination of the Sources to the Fifth Century A. D. and in the Epistle to the Hebrews* (1976), investigates the traditions about Melchizedek from the Old Testament onward through the first five centuries of the Christian era. He is concerned with tracing the growth and development of the tradition about Melchizedek, moving from his relatively minor position within the Old Testament to his divine status in some Jewish and early Christian texts.

The starting point of Horton's survey is a detailed exegesis of Genesis 14:18–20 and Psalm 110:4, the only two Old Testament texts that mention Melchizedek. He finds the theory that Melchizedek was a priest-king in Jerusalem before the Israelite conquest to be "weak on many sides" (p. 50). Moreover, he sees no grounding in these passages for taking the figure of Melchizedek as a divine redeemer. Philo treats Melchizedek as both a historical figure and a representative of the Logos, while Josephus observes that Melchizedek was the first priest (since he is the first person who is called a priest in the Torah).

In the Qumran scrolls Melchizedek is treated not only as a historical figure *(Genesis Apocryphon)* but also as a superior being of some sort who will appear at the end of days to bring atonement for the sons of light and who is the direct opponent of Belial (11QMelchizedek). The supernatural Melchizedek is said to judge "the holy ones of El" and to possess the name "Elohim" (one of the Hebrew names for God). The emphasis on Melchizedek as an angelic, eschatological figure in 11QMelchizedek is something on a different plane from how Melchizedek is portrayed by Philo, Josephus, and the *Genesis Apocryphon* (and Hebrews 7).

In some early Christian sources there are traces of the conviction that Melchizedek was a divine being who could be described as *theos* (divine, God). But his exact function varies according to the Christology of each system. In rabbinic sources Melchizedek is associated with the origins of the Levitical priesthood, as in some way the precursor of the Jewish priesthood. But no rabbinic text refers to Melchizedek as a divine or angelic being. In a few gnostic sources Melchizedek is a heavenly figure, though this development probably rests on a misreading of Hebrews 7 and on a tradition something like that preserved in 11QMelchizedek.

When Horton comes to interpret Hebrews 7, he too takes his starting point from Hebrews 7:3: "Without father, without mother, without genealogy...." He emphasizes that Melchizedek is the first priest mentioned in the Torah, that it would be natural to think of Jerusalem as the place of his priesthood (since Jerusalem became the one legitimate seat of sacrificial worship), and that the lack of genealogy underscores Melchizedek's originality as the first priest. Whereas the mainstream Jewish tradition found a transition from his priesthood to the Levitical priesthood, the author of Hebrews viewed Melchizedek's priesthood as the antitype of the higher priesthood of Christ. Horton concludes that Hebrews should not be reckoned with the literature in which Melchizedek is considered as a divine or heavenly figure. While granting that there are parallels between the Melchizedek of 11QMelchizedek and the Christ of Hebrews 7, he finds no direct connection or influence between the two texts.

In *Melchizedek and Melchiresha* (1981), **Paul Kobelski** gives a full study of the Qumran Melchizedek (and related) texts and is more positive than Horton is about their relevance for the study of Hebrews. In the first part Kobelski provides transcriptions, translations, and commentaries for 11QMelchizedek, 4Amram B (a description of dream visions), 4QTeharot D = 4Q280 1–2 (a series of curses that probably formed part of a Qumran Rule of Cleanness), and 4QBerakot A = 4Q286 10 ii 1=13 (part of a liturgical collection of blessings and curses). These texts mention Melchizedek as a heavenly figure and/or refer to Melchiresha as his evil counterpart.

The most important text is 11QMelchizedek, since it portrays Melchizedek as a priest, an Elohim (divine being), a king, and a judge. The most likely identification of Melchizedek in this text is the archangel Michael. While this figure is associated with the eschatological work of God, this does not demand that Melchizedek must be taken as another name for God. Rather, the references to Melchiresha in 4QAmram B and 4Q280 suggest that the two figures are two opposing angels otherwise known as the Prince of Light and the Prince of Darkness, as well as Michael and Belial, respectively. Kobelski traces this dualism to early Zoroastrian (Persian) ideas. He finds the Melchizedek/Melchiresha figures as pertinent for understanding the Paraclete passages in

John's Gospel and the glorious Son of Man texts in the Synoptic Gospels.

Kobelski regards 11QMelchizedek as useful for interpreting Hebrews 7 insofar as both texts present a heavenly Melchizedek. In 11QMelchizedek, Melchizedek's leadership over the angelic forces of light, his presence in the heavenly court to mete out God's judgment, and the reference to him as Elohim are evidence for his transcendent character and provide the basis for attributing eternal life to him. The Qumran text clarifies one of the key points in Hebrews 7: the priesthood of Melchizedek and Jesus as based on the power of indestructible life, not on the legal requirement of family descent. Nevertheless, the author of Hebrews insists on the superiority of Jesus. Kobelski concludes that while there is no evidence that the author of Hebrews was directly familiar with or even knew 11QMelchizedek, he was certainly familiar with a tradition about Melchizedek as a heavenly redeemer figure and made use of its elements in the description of Jesus.

The Hebrew word *Aqedah* (binding) is often used to describe the episode in Genesis 22:1–19 in which Abraham "binds" *('aqad)* his son Isaac (22:9) and lays him on the altar at Mount Moriah for sacrifice at God's command. The narrative is told in such a dramatic and suspenseful way that it has fascinated readers in antiquity and modern times. In *Jesus and Isaac: A Study of the Epistle to the Hebrews in the Light of the Aqedah* (1981), **James Swetnam** contends that the author of Hebrews thought about Jesus' death and resurrection in terms of the sacrifice of Isaac by Abraham as it is portrayed in Genesis 22 and as it was developed in later Jewish traditions.

After reviewing modern research on the Aqedah, Swetnam presents a comprehensive dossier of references to the sacrifice of Isaac in the Old Testament, early Jewish writings (Philo, Josephus, ps.-Philo's *Biblical Antiquities,* etc.) as well as rabbinic targums and midrashim, and the New Testament (especially Rom 8:32; Jas 2:21–22; Heb 11:17–19).

From these surveys Swetnam defines the Aqedah broadly as the totality of the events as they are represented in Genesis 22:1–19. He concludes that the Aqedah occupied an important place in Jewish traditions as a source of instruction and inspiration, was associated with the site of the Jerusalem temple in Jewish tradition, was generally regarded as involving a sacrifice (even though Isaac is rescued at the last minute), became associated with the vicarious expiation of sin through Jewish attempts to establish a theology of martyrdom and intensified by Jewish reactions to Christian claims about Christ, and eventually was linked with the New Year and Passover festivals.

Swetnam argues that the Aqedah tradition helps to explain key elements in the theology of Hebrews: the efficacy of Jesus' sacrifice over against Isaac's sacrifice, Jesus' offering himself to die, the role of shedding of blood in the expiation of sin, and the importance of spiritual descent from Abraham. He also maintains that several difficult passages in Hebrews are best understood when read against the background of the Aqedah.

The clearest reference to the Aqedah appears in Hebrews 11:17–19. There Abraham is said to have acted "by faith" when he was put to a test with God's command to sacrifice Isaac, the one through whom God's promises of offspring and the land were to be fulfilled. Swetnam contends that in Hebrews these promises are best interpreted "spiritually" and with reference to Christ. According to Hebrews 11:17–19, Abraham intended to sacrifice Isaac and tried to do so, and he received Isaac back by way of "foreshadowing" (literally, "parable") as a result of his faith in God's ability to raise Isaac from the dead. In Hebrews, the one who is preeminently offered and preeminently raised from the dead is Jesus.

Swetnam also finds the Aqedah to be the background of Hebrews 2:5–18 in its references to the "seed of Abraham," the Son of Man as "heir of all things" (see 1:2), Jesus' death and resurrection-exaltation, the theme of testing, the aspect of expiation, the mention of the devil in 2:14, and the use of Psalm 8 that was associated with the Aqedah in Jewish tradition.

The fact that the Aqedah helps to explain several other problematic texts in Hebrews bolsters Swetnam's case. In Hebrews 5:7–10, Jesus' pleading to die (rather than to avoid death) can be taken as influenced by the traditional Jewish motif of Isaac agreeing to die and even rejoicing at the prospect. Hebrews 6:13–15 insists that Abraham's faith and endurance at the sacrifice were not the cause of God's promises but rather a condition for the definitive granting of them in Christ. And in Hebrews 9:22 the emphasis given to the shedding of blood throws into sharp relief the view implied in 11:17–19 that the sacrifice of Isaac was incomplete and could not serve as a source of expiation for sin.

The catalogue of the heroes of faith in Hebrews 11 is a biblical text much loved by Christians. It provides the classic definition of faith in 11:1–2 and a long list of Old Testament examples involving many biblical figures. Its frequent repetition of the introductory formula "by faith" (11:3, 4, 5, 7, 8, etc.) makes for impressive public reading and achieves a powerful rhetorical effect. However, the careful reader may come away from Hebrews 11 with some basic questions: Why does the author choose these figures and not others? How cogent are the examples? and Why did the author omit some central and impressive demonstrations of biblical faith?

In *The Jewish Heroes of Christian Faith: Hebrews 11 in Literary Context* (1997), **Pamela M. Eisenbaum** takes up basic questions regarding content, background, and purpose and argues that in Hebrews 11 the author presents a distinctively Christian vision of Jewish religious history that focuses on "marginalized" individuals and offers a "de-nationalized" survey of ancient Israel's history.

Eisenbaum first places Hebrews 11 in the context of "hagiology" in antiquity; that is, lists of examples of great heroes and events in Jewish and Greco-Roman writings. She finds the closest analogues in Ben Sira's catalogue of "famous men" (Sir 44—50), the description of Wisdom's activity in ancient Israel's history (Wis 10), and the "sectarian" reading of biblical history in the *Damascus Document* (cols. 2—3). She also discovers pertinent comparative material in other Jewish texts and in Greek and Latin rhetorical treatises. Nevertheless, these comparisons only highlight the distinctive character of Hebrews 11, render unlikely hypotheses about the author's reliance on sources other than the Old Testament, and suggest that the author composed the passage to provide historical grounding for the community being addressed in Hebrews (the implied reader). The point seems to have been to show that if these persons could live a life of faith before Christ, how much more should those who live in the time of Christ be faithful.

Before her exposition of Hebrews 11, Eisenbaum distinguishes between the author's use of direct quotations of Scripture (which become oracles of God for the present) and his paraphrastic rendering of Scripture in narrative sections (which play down or devalue the Old Testament, especially with regard to the Sinai covenant and the promise of the land). This hermeneutic is part of the author's program to demonstrate the superiority of Christ and of the theological system that came into being as a result of his reign.

In her exposition, Eisenbaum contends that the "definition" of faith and the repetition of "by faith" are really rhetorical features, and that the author's primary goal was to provide a distinctively Christian reading of ancient Israel's history. She divides the chapter into six parts: introduction (11:1–3); primeval figures (11:4–7); pilgrim's promise — Abraham, Sarah, and the patriarchs (11:8–22); exodus and entropy — Moses, the Israelites, and Rahab (11:23–31); summary allusion to remaining history (11:32–38); and conclusion (11:39–40).

She argues that the heroes in Hebrews 11 are marginalized individuals who are portrayed as standing outside the nation of Israel. They are "strangers and exiles" always in search of their true (heavenly) home. In this framework the *telos* (goal) of biblical history is Jesus Christ and not the Sinai covenant or the land of

Israel. The author interprets the Old Testament not as the national history of the Jewish people but rather as the "pre-Christ" and "trans-ethnic" history of Christians. Such a reading of the Old Testament would have been most welcome among Gentile Christians, and its agenda of de-nationalizing Jewish Scripture marked a turning point in the early Christian appropriation of biblical history.

Biblical Texts

For most readers of Hebrews today the prologue in 1:1–4 ("Long ago God spoke...") makes their spirits soar, but the collection of seven biblical quotations that follows in chapter 1 leaves their minds puzzled and disoriented. These mysterious quotations come one after another, without context, identification, or much explanation. But given their prominent place at the very beginning of Hebrews, it is safe to assume that its first readers were expected to value and appreciate them.

In *Early Jewish Hermeneutics and Hebrews 1:5–13* (1997), **Herbert W. Bateman** seeks to catch glimpses of early Jewish biblical usage and interpretation and to compare those hermeneutical practices to the list of biblical quotations in Hebrews 1:5–13. His aim is to read the New Testament passage in the context of Second Temple Judaism and to show the distinctively Christian theological message that emerges from the application of these texts to Jesus Christ.

In the first part of his work Bateman explains some principles of early Jewish hermeneutics: from the lesser to the greater, verbal analogy from one verse to another, building a "family" of texts, and so forth. Then he focuses on three examples of Bible usage by Jews in Jesus' time and illustrates them mainly by texts discovered among the Dead Sea scrolls at Qumran: targums, or translations and paraphrases of biblical texts *(Targum of Job);* midrashim, or lists, expositions, and expansive explanations of biblical texts *(4QFlorilegium);* and pesharim, or eschatological revelations in the form of comments on biblical texts *(Pesher on Habakkuk)*. He contends that these three different uses of the Old Testament are not only literary genres but also literary-theological processes.

In the second part Bateman focuses on Hebrews 1:5–13. He first demonstrates that the author used a Greek text very much like the Septuagint but felt free to adapt and modify its wording in a few places to strengthen the theological argument he was making. Then he offers a detailed comparison between Hebrews 1:5–13 and *4QFlorilegium*. The word "florilegium" means the same as "anthology" and here refers to a collection of Old Testament quotations in a Hebrew manuscript found at Qumran. That work strings together texts from 2 Samuel 7:10–14 and elsewhere (Exod 15:17–18; Deut 23:3–4; Amos 9:11), and provides some introductory formulas and short comments. The effect of the Qumran collection is to present the profile of a future Davidic messiah who will one day come and rule over an eschatological sanctuary.

Hebrews 1:5–13 is much like *4QFlorilegium* in its literary form. It too is a collection of biblical quotations, plus minimal but significant commentary. However, the author of Hebrews has an even more ambitious theological program—to present Jesus as the divine Davidic king. By the seven quotations in 1:5–13 he wants to link Old Testament citations about a king (2 Sam 7:14; Pss 2:7; 45:6–7; 110:1b) with citations about Yahweh (Deut 32:43; Pss 102:25–27; 104:4). He wants to show that Jesus is superior to the prophets and kings of old and even to the angels, and that he is not only the Son of God but even worthy of language that is reserved for God alone in the Old Testament.

The result of Bateman's analysis of Hebrews 1:5–13 is an outline of the anthology in the form of a "conceptual chiasm." That is, there is center point around (1:8–9) which the other parts (A, B, B, A) revolve in a symmetrical way: A—the Son's status as Davidic king (Heb 1:5 = Ps 2:7; 2 Sam 7:14); B—the Son's status as God (Heb 1:6–7 = Deut 32:43; Ps 104:4); C—the Son's status as divine Davidic king (Heb 1:8–9 = Ps 45:6–7); B—the Son's status as God (Heb 1:10–12 = Ps 102:25–27); and A—the Son's status as Davidic king (Heb 1:13 = Ps 110:1).

One of the author's favorite biblical texts is Psalm 110, and within that psalm his favorite verse is Psalm 110:4: "You are a priest forever according to the order of Melchizedek." In *Jesus Our Priest: Ps 110,4 and the Substructure of Heb 5,1–7,28* (2000), **James Kurianal** explores the significance of this verse in the work's development of the concept of Christ as the high priest and in the structure of Hebrews as a whole. He contends that Hebrews 5:1—7:28 highlights the uniqueness of Christ the new high priest: The new high priest is the Son of God, and the agent declaring him as high priest is God himself. The use of Psalm 110:4 marks off the passage as an embedded discourse unit and provides a key to the substructure of 5:1—7:28 and the structure of Hebrews as a whole.

Kurianal characterizes Psalm 110 as a royal psalm that was regarded as messianic from the early Christian period onward. It consists first of an oracle or promise from Yahweh (110:1–4), and then of a description of how the promise was (to be) realized (110:5–7). The first use of Psalm 110:4 in Hebrews appears in 5:1–10, which Kurianal takes to be the beginning of a new unit in Hebrews and the first part of an "inclusion" formed with 7:1–28 to mark off an embedded unit in the text. Indeed, a major part of Kurianal's task is to show that the uses of Psalm 110:4 serve as "bookends" for the unit that is at the core of the argument in Hebrews.

Within Hebrews 5:1–10, according to Kurianal, there are two subsections: 5:1–4, which gives the qualifications for the levitical high priesthood, and 5:5–10, which reflects on the relationship of Christ's sonship and incarnation to his priesthood. Contrary to the opinion of most exegetes, Kurianal finds the high priestly qualifications taken up not in 5:5–10 but rather in 7:1–28, after the exhortation in 5:11—6:20.

Kurianal interprets Hebrews 7:1–25, a three-part midrash on Psalm 110:4b: "You are a priest forever according to the order of

Melchizedek." In 7:1–10 the author establishes the superiority of "Melchizedek" over the Levitical priests, with particular attention to Melchizedek as the one who lives without end and remains a priest in perpetuity. In 7:11–19 the key word is "order," and the main idea is that Jesus becoming a priest means a change in the order of the priesthood and therefore proves that the Levitical priesthood could not provide perfection. The third section (7:20–25) emphasizes the eternal nature (forever) of the new priest and of the new covenant of which Christ is the guarantor. Hebrews 7:26–28 serves not as the continuation of the argument but rather as the solemn conclusion to the argument developed in 5:1 – 7:25. It affirms that Jesus has become a high priest according to the order of Melchizedek, and that he is a better high priest than the Levitical high priests were.

Where did the author of Hebrews get these ideas? Not from Philo or from various Qumran texts, but from general principles of Jewish exegesis and especially from his Christian faith in Jesus as the Son of God who is the savior. For Kurianal, the priesthood of Christ is not a simple continuation of the Levitical priesthood, nor did the priesthood of Melchizedek provide a complete blueprint for the priesthood of Christ. The real link between Melchizedek and Christ is their eternal character ("having neither beginning of days nor end of life," 7:3). The most prominent characteristics of Christ the high priest are that he is both human and eternal, an effective intercessor, and one who has been made perfect through suffering.

Only in Hebrews are Psalm 110:1 ("The Lord says to my lord: 'Sit at my right hand until I make your enemies your footstool'") and Psalm 110:4 ("The Lord has sworn and will not change his mind, 'You are a priest forever according to the order of Melchizedek'") used in the same New Testament writing. Psalm 110:1 is directly quoted once (Heb 1:13) and alluded to five times (1:3; 8:1; 10:12–13; 12:2), while Psalm 110:4 is quoted three times (5:6; 7:17; 7:21) and alluded to three times (5:10; 6:20; 7:3).

In *The King-Priest of Psalm 110 in Hebrews* (2001), **David R. Anderson** argues that the author of Hebrews used Psalm 110 to demonstrate that "there has been and only will be one King-Priest in the history and future of Israel" (p. 297), and that this unique priest is Jesus Christ. He maintains that Christ the King-Priest reigns in the present (already) and points forward to the fulfillment of God's promises to physical/spiritual Israel in the future (not yet).

In reviewing the evidence for "sacral kingship" (that is, when the king functions also as the priest) in the ancient Near East, Anderson contends that at least in the case of ancient Israel this is a dubious proposal. He regards Psalm 110 as having been written during David's reign, either by him or by a court prophet, and classifies it as a messianic psalm in which the Lord predicts the ultimate triumph of the messianic King-Priest over all his enemies. Elsewhere in the New Testament, Psalm 110 serves to establish Jesus' messiahship and second coming (Gospels), to support his messiahship and authority (Acts), and to emphasize the already/not yet dialectical view of eschatology (Paul, Peter).

Anderson stresses the role of Psalm 110:1 in Hebrews 1:3 and 1:13 in presenting Jesus as the Son promised to David (see Ps 2 and 2 Sam 7). The Son has inaugurated the Davidic kingdom as signified by his exaltation to the right hand of his Father in heaven. His kingdom has already begun because his enemies have been placed under his footstool. But the total, complete defeat of his enemies awaits the consummation of his kingdom. The concentrated use of Psalm 110:4 in Hebrews 5—7, along with four more allusions to Psalm 110:1, serves to show that the Melchizedekian priest and the Davidic Son are one and the same person, Jesus Christ. There are two offices but only one person. Jesus has a priesthood in perpetuity, and Psalm 110:4 is the *sine qua non* of Christ's priesthood and the cornerstone of the high priestly Christology that is central to Hebrews. The juxtaposition of Psalm 110:1 and 110:4 with Psalm 2 in Hebrews indicates that the priestly ministry of intercession began for Christ at his enthronement, and that his priesthood lasts forever in contrast to that of the Levites.

. There is general agreement that the Bible (what Christians call the Old Testament) that the author of Hebrews read and worked with in composing his own work was in Greek (generally known as the Septuagint). In *The Role of the Septuagint in Hebrews* (2003), **Radu Gheorghita** observes that the author of Hebrews based his word of exhortation solely on the Greek Scriptures without recourse to a Hebrew text. And so Gheorghita explores the extent to which the exclusive use of the Greek Bible, especially where it differs from the Hebrew text, may have influenced the language and theology of Hebrews.

In the first part of his study, Gheorghita examines the possible influences of the Greek Septuagint on Hebrews in five basic areas: quoting directly from Greek biblical texts, exploiting the context in which the texts appear in the Septuagint, basing biblical allusions on material found in the Septuagint, reflecting phrases or lexical units in the Greek Bible, and taking cues from the theology in the Septuagint (especially in the areas of eschatology and messianism).

In the second part, Gheorghita takes as a test case the use of Habakkuk 2:3–4 in Hebrews 10:37–38. He focuses on this particular text because it represents the most extensive editorial reshaping of any of the biblical quotations in the Epistle, and because it strengthens the case for the Septuagint's direct and distinct contribution to the textual form of the quotation in Hebrews. He examines its use in Hebrews in terms of text, context, and theology. He notes that the changes that the Hebrew original underwent through translation into Greek created an important biblical passage with the potential of expressing a crucial messianic idea within an eschatological framework.

Gheorghita concludes that the author's reliance on the Greek version of the Old Testament has produced an epistle whose argument at several junctures can be explained only by use of the Septuagint textual tradition, and that recourse to a Hebrew textual tradition would have resulted in a work quite different from the one that we now possess. He contends that the Septuagint supplied not only an authoritative confirmation of the new Christian message but also a suitable framework in which the new message could be delivered, thus admirably fulfilling its role as Scripture for the author of Hebrews.

Evaluation

No New Testament book contains such a sustained engagement with the Old Testament as Hebrews. Yet the author's interest is not so much exegetical as it is christological and theological. He views the Old Testament as an authoritative vehicle for advancing his Christian theological program. His treatment of the biblical texts is rooted firmly in Jewish interpretive traditions but even more firmly rooted in early Christian theology and in the author's distinctive theological genius.

The two general studies on the use of the Old Testament in Hebrews come from different critical perspectives but end up somewhat close in their insistence on the necessity of the Old Testament as a theological source and on its basic continuity with the Christ-event. Graham Hughes begins from the author's emphasis on superiority of the new covenant over the old covenant and its institutions. But Hughes concludes that the author was a creative exegete who struggles honestly with the Old Testament and arrives at a reading that is both true to Christian faith and respectful of the biblical texts and of the traditions associated with them. Dale Leschert begins from specific texts in the Psalms and argues that what the author of Hebrews does with them is never a distortion of their biblical meaning but rather is always at least consonant with their intended sense according to historical-grammatical hermeneutics. In both books there is some vagueness about what constitutes the original or literal sense of the biblical texts. But they do agree that the author's Christ-centered hermeneutical stance, while not inevitable, does not necessarily distort or twist the meaning of the Old Testament passages that he interprets.

The investigations of how various biblical characters—Moses (Mary Rose D'Angelo), Melchizedek (Bruce Demarest, Fred Horton, Paul Kobelski), Isaac (James Swetnam), and the heroes of faith in chapter 11 (Pamela Eisenbaum)—are treated in Hebrews reveal that there is more to the author's biblical hermeneutics than simply quoting and interpreting texts. Rather, the presentations of these figures in Hebrews are the result of a sophisticated combination of key Old Testament passages, Jewish exegetical traditions, early Christian beliefs about Jesus, and the author's own creative theological vision.

The tradition-historical studies of Moses and Isaac in Hebrews compile impressive dossiers of comparative materials and bring them to bear on some parts of Hebrews. The discovery and publication of 11QMelchizedek set off another round in the debate about Hebrews and the Dead Sea scrolls. But the discussion ended in something of a "draw," with Horton representing a minimalist view and Kobelski the maximalist position that Jewish traditions about Melchizedek as a heavenly figure may have influenced the author of Hebrews. Eisenbaum's study of Hebrews 11 is quite successful in marshaling comparative materials, clarifying the author's redactional and theological concerns, and answering some difficult questions about the passage.

Herbert Bateman's investigation of the anthology of biblical texts in Hebrews 1:5–13 illustrates the extent to which the work must be understood with reference to Jewish parallels (in this case *4QFlorilegium,* an anthology from Qumran) and at the same time recognized as a thoroughly Christian text with a very high Christology. Likewise, the two monographs devoted to Psalm 110 by James Kurianal and David Anderson indicate how pivotal that psalm is to the structure and content of Hebrews, and how it serves to support some very exalted statements about Jesus

Christ. The "Old Testament" used in Hebrews is the Greek version known as the Septuagint. The analysis by Radu Gheorghita highlights the need for attending to the points at which the Septuagint texts differ from the Hebrew Masoretic version as a way of better appreciating the biblical roots of some of the author's distinctive theological interests.

4
The Theology of Hebrews

"Since, then, we have a great high priest who has passed
through the heavens, Jesus, the Son of God, let us hold fast
to our confession." (Heb 4:14)

While Hebrews is of interest on the literary and historical
levels, it is most significant for its theology. The author stands
beside Paul and John as one of the great theologians of the New
Testament. His work is an in-depth exposition of the early Christian confession of faith: "Christ died for our sins in accordance
with the scriptures" (1 Cor 15:3).

The basic theological thesis of Hebrews is that Christ's suffering and death constituted the one perfect sacrifice for sins, and
that because Christ went willingly to his death he can be regarded
as the great high priest. Thus Christ is both the one perfect sacrifice for sins and the priest who offers that sacrifice.

Barnabas Lindars has provided a fine synthesis of the distinctive theology of Hebrews, its relationships to other theologies
in the New Testament, and its significance for Christian theology
and life today. Various aspects of the theology of Hebrews have
been clarified in recent years not only in the commentaries but
also in monographs devoted to such themes as wandering and
rest, priesthood and sacrifice, perfection, the new covenant,
sacred space, suffering, and faith.

General Survey

The late **Barnabas Lindars**, an Anglican Franciscan and professor at the University of Manchester, was highly competent in both Old Testament and New Testament studies and was especially interested in the use of the Old Testament in the New Testament. Thus he was an ideal candidate to write *The Theology of the Letter to the Hebrews* (1991) for the New Testament Theology series.

While describing Hebrews as full of theology and its author as one of the three great theologians of the New Testament (along with Paul and John), Lindars insists that Hebrews is not a theological treatise but rather a pastoral letter designed to convince wavering Jewish Christians about the complete and abiding efficacy of Jesus' death as an atoning sacrifice. Although he admits some influence from Hellenistic Judaism, he contends that the chief influence on the author's thought was mainstream Christian life and teaching. According to Lindars, the portrayal of Christ in Hebrews was deeply indebted to the primitive Christian kerygma with regard to Jesus' pre-existence, exaltation as Messiah and Son of God, relation to the angels, humanity, and saving death.

Nevertheless, the author of Hebrews was also an original and creative Christian theologian in many areas. The "perfection" that Christ attains according to Hebrews belongs to his completing the divine plan or purpose (*telos*). The use of the Old Testament provided him with an agreed standard that the first readers accepted as authoritative as well as a metaphorical basis for his argument. In Hebrews 5 — 10, three great strands come together. First, the priesthood according to the order of Melchizedek qualifies Jesus the Messiah to perform the sacrifice that is required for atonement for sins. Second, the eschatological concept of the inauguration of the new covenant gives Jesus' sacrificial death its permanent efficacy because it opens the era of salvation in which fresh sacrifices for sin are no longer required. Third, the model of the Day of Atonement provided the essential requirements for an atoning sacrifice which are fulfilled in the sacrificial death of Jesus.

Lindars contends that the author of Hebrews was writing primarily for Jewish Christians who were doubting that their sins had really been forgiven. In this context "faith" is both the proper response to the sacrifice of Christ and the human side in the new covenant. Faith is a moral quality that should be constantly expressed in Christian living. Following Jesus as the pioneer and perfecter of faith (12:2), Christians live in the present in the light of the future because the completion of God's plan of salvation has already been reached in the person of Jesus, though it still waits to be completed at his parousia.

While describing Hebrews as a unique strand within the New Testament, Lindars also contends that it shares much with other New Testament writings. It shares the free attitude toward the Law and the Temple found in Stephen's speech in Acts 7, a Wisdom Christology (compare 1:1–4 and Col 1:15–20), the confession that Christ died for our sins, and the already/not yet eschatology. What is distinctive or even unique in Hebrews are the long and sustained arguments (comparable only to Paul's letter to the Romans), explicit statements of Christian supersessionism (better covenant, priesthood, sacrifice, etc. than those of Judaism), the sustained and creative use of Scripture in the argument, the emphasis on the permanent efficacy of Jesus' sacrificial death (once for all), the priesthood of Jesus, the Church as the pilgrim people of God, and faith as action in the light of assurance concerning the future divine judgment.

By way of conclusion Lindars points to features in Hebrews that many people today may find foreign and/or problematic: its christocentric exclusivism, apparently artificial use of Scripture, taking sacrifice as the central category, and rigorist approach to post-baptismal sin. Its positive contributions lay especially in its strong emotional appeal, and in its emphasis on Christ as the pioneer and perfecter of our faith (12:2) and on the pastoral nature of his priesthood. With regard to the Christian ministerial priesthood, Lindars notes that Hebrews has been used both to affirm and to deny the legitimacy of that concept, primarily because the text never really addresses the topic.

Wandering and Rest

In Hebrews 3:7—4:11 the author gives a long quotation of Psalm 95:7–11 and then contrasts the rebellious and fruitless wanderings of the exodus generation in the wilderness with the journey of Christians as God's people on their way with the risen Christ as their leader to perfect rest with God in heaven. The thesis of **Ernst Käsemann**'s *The Wandering People of God: An Investigation of the Letter to the Hebrews* (1984) is that the theme of the wandering people of God runs through and unifies all of Hebrews. The last sentence in his book neatly summarizes the argument: "all the utterances in Hebrews culminate in the description of Christ's high priestly office, but take their basis, which supports and purposefully articulates the individual parts, from the motif of the wandering people of God" (p. 240).

Although the English version of Käsemann's work appeared only in 1984, the German original was written in 1937 while Käsemann was in jail for preaching against National Socialism (Nazism) and the "German Christians" (who actively supported the Nazis). Käsemann (1906-98) became a famous New Testament scholar and wrote many influential books and articles. His status as an academic theologian was such that it was fitting that his early monograph on Hebrews be made available in English for a new generation.

Käsemann's work on Hebrews stands up well in its theology but not in its history. Taking Hebrews 3:7—4:13 as his point of departure, Käsemann describes the wandering people of God as the bearer of the revelation of God's word, and in that context he explains the author's distinctive approaches to key theological terms such as "promise," "faith," "sin," "worship," and "witness." Then he explores the relationship between Jesus as the

"Son of God" and Christians as the "sons of God": "the redeemed become sons of God only because they first become sons or children of the redeemer" (p. 148). Finally he shows how the basis for the wandering people of God's ultimate certainty of redemption is disclosed in the activity of Jesus as the heavenly high priest. For the Christian community, the message of the high priestly activity of the exalted one spells the certainty (and so the hope) of salvation even in the face of its weaknesses.

The problem on the historical level is Käsemann's adoption of an approach to Christians origins that was popular among some German Protestant scholars before World War II but is now rejected by practically everyone. According to this approach that had its roots in the "history of religions school" in the early years of the twentieth century, gnosticism was a pre-Christian phenomenon that promoted the myth of the primal human being and of the "redeemed redeemer." For those scholars (including the younger Käsemann) early Hellenistic Christians took over so many elements of the gnostic myth that much of the New Testament is unintelligible without recourse to it. But the literary sources on which these theories were built by modern scholars were written well after the New Testament, and there is little or no evidence for gnosticism or the redeemed redeemer myth in pre-Christian times.

The main problem with Käsemann's monograph is that its incisive and challenging theological insights (which are especially admirable in the historical context in which he wrote) are tied at every point to what has become an indefensible historical hypothesis about Christian origins in general and about Hebrews in particular. Nevertheless, his book remains worth reading today for its treatment of a central theme in Hebrews and for its profound theological and homiletical comments.

The goal of the journey undertaken by the wandering people of God in the exodus generation was rest in the land of Canaan. But because of their disobedience and unbelief, according to Psalm 95:7–11, they failed to attain their goal of rest. In *'I Will*

Give You Rest': The Rest Motif in the New Testament with Special Reference to Mt 11 and Heb 3—4 (1997), **Jon Laansma** shows that both Matthew 11:28–30 and Hebrews 3:7—4:11 envisage a fulfillment of specific Old Testament themes of rest in Christ.

Laansma distinguishes two strands associated with the theme of rest in the Old Testament: the Deuteronomistic ideas of Israel's rest in the land of Canaan and Yahweh's rest in the temple, and the Sabbath rest linked to God's rest on the seventh day of creation and to the hope for the eschatological Sabbath rest. In both cases rest is a redemptive category. From the Septuagint version of Genesis 2:2–3 ("God rested") the Greek term *katapausis* (rest) became part of the biblical rest tradition. Moreover, in early Jewish literature the hope for rest or for entrance into a resting place was increasingly projected into the ultimate future, possibly even into another (upper or future) world, and often into postmortem existence.

Rejecting the common interpretation of Jesus' promise of rest in Matthew 11:28–29 ("I will give you rest…you will find rest") in terms of Wisdom, Laansma argues that Matthew has Jesus utter this saying as the Son of David who claims to bring to fulfillment Yahweh's promise of rest to his people. Key to this interpretation is 2 Samuel 7:11, a part of Nathan's message from God to David: "and I will give you rest from all your enemies." Despite their many differences, Laansma contends that both Matthew and the author of Hebrews were primarily interested in drawing on the Old Testament promises and imagery of rest as a soteriological symbol for expressing the absence of the hoped-for salvation.

Laansma describes Hebrews 3:7—4:11 as an extended exhortation to listen before the argument turns to the exposition of Christ's priestly ministry. The linking of Psalm 95:7–11 with Genesis 2:2–3 in Hebrews 4:1–11 indicates that the resting place is where God holds his Sabbath celebration, that this resting place was always intended for human entrance and was promised to the "fathers," that this promise will be realized only with the obedience on the part of those who receive it, and that entrance into this resting place will involve joining into God's Sabbath celebration by resting from one's own works.

The main pastoral concern of Hebrews 4:1–11, according to Laansma, was that since the fullness of salvation is essentially future, believers are on probation until it (the parousia) arrives. The promised rest is construed as a locale, as God's own resting place, where he celebrates his own Sabbath. Laansma describes the author of Hebrews as an independent Hellenistic Jewish Christian thinker, contends that Hebrews 4:1–11 is best viewed as an independent Christian midrash on Psalm 95:7–11 and Genesis 2:2–3, and maintains that its most distinctive features probably arose from the author's own christological and paraenetic concerns as they were brought to bear on those biblical passages.

In *Rest as a Theological Metaphor in the Epistle to the Hebrews and the Gospel of Truth: Early Christian Homiletics of Rest* (1998), **Judith Hoch Wray** looks at the metaphor of rest as it is used rhetorically in order to add to our understanding of how rest is understood theologically in Hebrews and the *Gospel of Truth,* a second-century Valentinian gnostic text. Both works can be described as homilies or sermons, and Wray is especially interested in how rest functions homiletically in each text.

Wray first examines the Greek terms *katapausis* and *anapausis,* notes the influence of the Septuagint version of Genesis 2:2–3 ("God rested") in both Jewish and Christian traditions, and charts the development of the metaphor of rest in six steps: rest as land, as Sabbath practice, as eschatological expectation, as existential possibility, as salvific state of being, and as matrix for a comprehensive theological system.

Wray regards Hebrews 3:7 — 4:13 as a short sermon within the large sermon of Hebrews as a whole. She considers 3:1–6 (Jesus the faithful Son over God's house) and 4:14 (Jesus as the Son of God) as thesis statements that demarcate the short sermon. After quoting Psalm 95:7–11 in 3:7–11, the author presents an argument and an exposition about the danger of unfaithfulness in 3:12–19, draws a conclusion and offers a discourse on entering into rest in 4:1–10, and gives an exhortation on striving to enter into that rest in 4:11–13.

The author of Hebrews, according to Wray, understood rest in the context of God's own rest in the primordial sabbath of creation (see Gen 2:2–3). While aware of eschatological realities, the author sought to inspire faithfulness in the community "today." Wray observes that rest, entering into the rest, and the threat of failing to enter the rest form a powerful homiletical element in a carefully crafted rhetoric of encouragement. However, Wray admits that Hebrews 3:7 — 4:13 says more about what rest is not than about what rest is. Nevertheless, she does venture a definition of entering into rest as "a to-be-maintained participation in the completed cosmic work of God" (p. 91). She notes that in Hebrews 3:7 — 4:13 rest is a reward for faithfulness but is not yet defined as an integral result of participation in Christ.

By way of development (and contrast) Wray investigates the mid-second century *Gospel of Truth* in which rest becomes the defining metaphor for salvation in the past, present, and future. In the *Gospel of Truth* rest is the place, the locus of God's presence, from which God acts and redemption goes forth. Rest is also, for the believer, that state of being characterized in the present by tranquility and peace, by lack of stress as a result of knowledge of one's place in the unity, in the Father.

Examination of references to rest in other early Christian texts (Matt 11:28–30; *Epistle of Barnabas* 15; and *2 Clement*) leads Wray to conclude that while in early Christian communities there was no consensus about a doctrine of rest, the short sermon presented in Hebrews 3:7 — 4:13 opened the way for further Christian development of the theological metaphor of rest.

Priesthood and Sacrifice

While the author of Hebrews gives abundant attention to the priesthood of Christ, he is less (if at all) insistent on the priesthood of all Christians. In 1 Peter 2:5, Christians are addressed as "a holy priesthood," and in Revelation (1:6; see also 5:10; 20:6), they are described as "priests" serving God. Whether a similar understanding of Christian life can be found in Hebrews (that is, the priestly status of the readers) is the topic of **John M. Scholer**'s *Proleptic Priests: Priesthood in the Epistle to the Hebrews* (1991). Scholer emphasizes that any claim to priesthood on the part of Christians must flow from the high priesthood of Christ. He contends that since believers are already enjoying access to God through Jesus' death and exaltation and are offering sacrifices of praise, worship, and thanksgiving now in the "end-time days," and all the while they are anticipating the eschatological future when full and direct access to God in heaven will be enjoyed, they can legitimately be described as "proleptic priests" in that they enjoy now and look forward to what is the essence of priesthood—access to God.

The author of Hebrews, along with Jewish writers of his time, took his basic understanding of priesthood from the Old Testament, though his concept of Christians as proleptic priests may owe something to efforts at the "spiritualizing" of the biblical priesthood in some Qumran texts and Philo's writings. However, the major influence seems to have been early Christian confessions about Jesus' death "for us" and "for our sins" and about the high priesthood of Christ who sacrificed himself as a priest in order to sanctify his brothers and sisters (2:10–18; 9:13–14; 10:10, 14, 29; 13:12). As their "forerunner" (6:19–20), Christ anticipated accessibility for the people of God to the heavenly holy of holies.

Central to Scholer's case for Christians as proleptic priests in Hebrews is the analysis of three Greek verbs that appear frequently in sacral contexts: *proserchesthai* (draw near), *eiserchesthai* (enter), and *teleioun* (complete, reach a goal). All three verbs derive their theological meaning in Hebrews from their use in connection with the prior activity of Jesus as the truly effective high priest who entered the heavenly holy of holies and thus achieved his goal of opening up full access to God.

The author uses *proserchesthai* in this context to refer to the spiritual inner access to heaven that the Christian community has while still residing on earth. Likewise, the aorist uses of *eiserchesthai* emphasize the necessity of their own death before Christians can gather around the throne in heaven, seeing God in part and offering the same worship of prayer and praise as those who draw near on earth. The two verbs converge in *teleioun,* which describes attaining the goal which is the direct presence of God—the goal that Christ has already attained. Because Christians are still alive and have not yet attained their goal of perfect access to God, their priesthood is proleptic (that is, by way of anticipation). While believers in the present enjoy access to God and offer their sacrifices of praise, worship, and thanksgiving, all the while they anticipate the eschatological future when full and direct access to God will be enjoyed.

In *Covenant and sacrifice in the Letter to the Hebrews* (1992), **John Dunnill** offers a holistic reading of Hebrews through the medium of its sacrificial symbolism that draws extensively on social anthropology in general and structuralism in particular. The value of structuralism as an interpretive tool is that it helps us to see the Old Testament cultus and Hebrews as integrated wholes rather than as bundles of contingent particulars. Dunnill's basic thesis is that Hebrews claims for itself the image of a liturgy (a symbolic action in the sacred sphere) and more particularly a covenant-renewal rite of which the book's words comprise a long prophetic exhortation.

Dunnill describes Hebrews as an encyclical letter addressed to a series of small churches of predominantly Jewish Christians, most probably in western Asia Minor. Their members seem to be suffering persecution from outside and disillusionment and doubt from within. The author wants to show them that the true house of God is not a palace or dynasty or temple or priesthood but the community identified with Christ as both priest and king, whose palace and sanctuary are in heaven.

To appreciate the theology of Hebrews, one must first understand the system of sacrifice and covenant in the Old Testament. The priestly redactors of the Torah shaped various elements in ancient Israel's ritual life into what approaches being a coherent system. At the heart of this system is the act of sacrifice which takes several forms (communion, participation, propitiation, expiation/aversion) and reflects different conceptions about God (personal, impersonal) and God's relationship to humans (conjunctive, disjunctive). The sacrificial system is the foundation on which the priesthood and the temple are built, and all takes place under the canopy of God's covenantal relationship with Israel. In this context the Day of Atonement and the sprinkling of animal blood in the Holy of Holies to wipe away the people's sins are central.

According to Dunnill, the author of Hebrews alone among the New Testament writers attempts a systematic interpretation of Christian salvation as fulfillment of the Old Testament sacrificial cultus. Its central argument expounds the death and exaltation of Jesus as the fulfillment of the Day of Atonement ritual and in particular of the entry of the high priest into the Holy of Holies. In its references to Old Testament characters (Abel, Abraham and Isaac, Moses, Rahab, etc.) and events (the "sacrifice" of Isaac in Genesis 22, the Passover, and the exodus), it reveals God to be both fearful and graciously approachable.

In fulfilling his role as Abraham's son and entering into death, Jesus offers a way of resolving the tension between the mercy and mercilessness of God. The blood of Jesus is better than the blood of the old covenant in being human blood, voluntarily offered, and embracing a moral as well as a ritual dimension. The language of sacrifice, for Dunnill, provides a coherent and nuanced vocabulary for setting out the cosmology of Hebrews, encompassing creation, evil, and the human nature within the framework of salvation.

While rooted in the expiatory sacrifice of the Day of Atonement, the sacrifice of Christ has even more the effect of a communion in making available access to and fellowship with God through Christ. Now true worship is possible at every time ("today") and in every place (not confined to the Jerusalem temple). The media of this worship are various forms of direct communion, supplication, intercession, promises, and blessing. There is now no need for priests or Eucharists, according to Dunnill, since all mediation is now exercised by Jesus Christ.

In some evangelical Protestant circles the terms "cultus" (in the sense of religious ritual) and "spirituality" are suspect. However, in *The Cultic Motif in the Spirituality of the Book of Hebrews* (1993), **Darrell J. Pursiful** contends that the cultic motif in the spirituality of Hebrews is intricate, imaginative, and everywhere present. He argues that in this masterful sermon the author of Hebrews consistently pointed beyond the cultus that had long been the center of his audience's spiritual life to Jesus Christ as the single focus. As Pursiful states: "Through the language of ritual and priesthood and sanctuary he bids us all to root our spiritualities in the story of Jesus' death and resurrection" (p. 175).

Pursiful defines cultus as "a system of visible and culturally established religious acts or symbols conceived as a coherent whole" (p. 12). And he takes a wide view of spirituality as including "all that has to do with giving expression to one's commitment to God" (pp. 13–14). He regards Hebrews as a sermon written by a Christian of Hellenistic-Jewish origin to and for a house church at Rome in the 60s of the first century. He adopts the methods of historical-critical exegesis, phenomenology of religion, anthropology, and the academic study of spirituality.

According to Pursiful, what links the "Old Covenant Cultus" and the "Christ Cultus" are their common recognition of the need for a mediator and their belief in the effectiveness of blood for cleansing from sin. But the Christ Cultus is superior to the Old Covenant Cultus in giving direct access to the divine, in cleansing even the conscience of worshipers, and in providing a cultus

(Jesus' priesthood, sanctuary, and liturgy) of heavenly value. The result is that Jesus is the center of spirituality for Hebrews.

The treatment of the "Heavenly Cultus" in which the angels participate reinforces the emphasis in Hebrews on a Christ-centered spirituality. The "New Covenant Cultus" in which Christians on earth participate constitutes a spiritualization of the cultic institutions of the Old Covenant Cultus in the sense of going to their inner spiritual or ethical significance. The New Covenant Cultus need not take the form of material sacrifices, since Jesus' death and exaltation have rendered them unnecessary. Rather, Christian spirituality now revolves around engaging in corporate worship, making everyday life into a spiritual sacrifice, doing good works, and letting go of the past.

Indeed, Pursiful regards Hebrews as written to deal with the crisis of spirituality precipitated by his audience's separation from their traditional forms of religion. While Jesus' death in its historical facticity was not a cultic act, the author of Hebrews imported into this event a fully developed interpretation based almost exclusively on cultic categories. Jesus' death is presented as the perfect sacrifice of the great high priest in the heavenly sanctuary. In turn the saving work of Jesus makes it possible to view Christian existence as a cultic performance.

Those who read Hebrews today are often puzzled by the fact that the author speaks not directly about the Jerusalem Temple but rather about the "tabernacle," the portable shrine that according to the Pentateuch was the place where ancient Israelites worshiped God and offered sacrifices from the days of Moses until the building of the Jerusalem Temple under King Solomon. **David's M. Levy**'s *The Tabernacle: Shadows of the Messiah* (2003), provides basic information (with excellent illustrations) about the tabernacle, sacrifices, and priesthood in ancient Israel. As Levy notes, while only two chapters in the Bible are devoted to describing the creation of the world, fifty chapters concern the tabernacle and its related ministries. And among the several reasons for studying these chapters, one is that "a good grasp of the Tabernacle is necessary to understand more than half of the book of Hebrews" (p. 8).

Levy's work is not a scholarly book like the others treated in this volume. Intended for the general public and with a strong Christian evangelistic bent, it presents readings of the pertinent biblical texts and many splendid photographs and drawings. The photographs of the tabernacle as it has been reconstructed by members of Kibbutz Almog at Timna Park in Israel are especially helpful in enabling readers of Hebrews to visualize what the author of Hebrews is talking about.

Levy treats the structure of the tabernacle and its furnishings, the sacrificial system and the various kinds of sacrifices (burnt, meal, peace, sin, and trespass offerings), and the priesthood (qualifications, clothing, consecration, and service) in ancient Israel. The presentation of this material leads Levy into reflections on Christ "as the only high priest suitable to officiate before God on behalf of sinful mankind" (p. 180) and on the tabernacle described in the Torah as "only a shadow of the real sanctuary in heaven" (p. 190). While not an objective scholarly treatment, Levy's book can help readers of Hebrews today to develop the historical imagination (especially by way of the illustrations) that is necessary to appreciate the arguments about Christ's priesthood and sacrifice according to Hebrews.

Other Themes

In *Hebrews and Perfection* (1982), David Peterson contends that the Greek verb *teleioun* (perfect) and related terms are central to the argument of Hebrews. He argues that the author was seeking to deal with a problem of spiritual lethargy on the part of his readers, involving loss of zeal, lack of confidence, and faltering hope. They were most likely Jewish Christians who were tempted to slip back into a form of Judaism in order to escape the hostility and suffering associated with being Christians. The author's response was to invite them to consider again "Jesus, the apostle and high priest of our confession" (3:1) and to concentrate on Jesus' person and achievement on their behalf. In this program the theme of perfection plays a major role.

Investigation of the linguistic background of *teleioun* and related terms in classical Greek sources, the Septuagint, the New Testament, and early Christian literature leads Peterson to emphasize the general or formal sense of "make perfect, complete, accomplish, fulfill" — a meaning strongly influenced by the cognate noun *telos* (goal, end, purpose). He finds no specific moral or religious connotation consistently attached to the term. And so he proposes that the most valid approach to its uses in Hebrews is to determine the content always with reference to the context.

In three places (2:10; 5:9; 7:28) Hebrews refers to the perfecting of Christ, and in all three cases it is a matter of Christ fulfilling and bringing his vocation as Son of God and great high priest to its goal. In the context of Hebrews 2:5–18 the perfecting of Christ ("it was fitting that God…should make the pioneer of their salvation perfect through sufferings") involves a whole sequence of events: his testing in suffering, his redemptive death to fulfill the divine requirements for the perfect expiation of sins, and his exaltation to glory and honor. In the context of Hebrews 4:14 — 5:10 the perfecting of Christ ("having been made perfect, he became the source of eternal salvation for all who obey him") reflects the earthly struggle that Christ underwent in fulfilling his vocation as high priest to be in sympathy with other humans and to carry out his task as Servant of the Lord. In the context of Hebrews 7:1–28, the perfecting of Christ ("a Son who has been made perfect forever") refers to the significance of his heavenly exaltation for himself and his people: The immediate context in 7:26–28 suggests the importance of the whole process of Jesus' testing, his self-sacrifice in obedience to the Father, and his heavenly exaltation for his perfecting as high priest after the order of Melchizedek.

On four occasions in Hebrews (7:11, 19; 9:9; 10:1) we are told that the old covenant ritual was unable to "perfect" the worshippers. On three occasions (10:14; 11:40; 12:23) we are told that Christ alone is the source of perfection for believers, though the use of related terms elsewhere in Hebrews proclaims the same truth. Moreover, the author urges his readers on to spiritual maturity in 5:11—6:1 and points them to Christ as the "perfecter" of faith in 12:2. In all the occurrences of "perfection" in Hebrews what is crucial is the vocational sense; that is, the idea that Christ (and those who believe in him) is made perfect by fulfilling his calling and so reaching his *telos* (goal, end, purpose).

For most Christians, the new covenant is a familiar concept. They may hear it regularly at celebrations of the Eucharist in which it is part of "the words of institution" based on 1 Corinthians 11:25 (see Luke 22:20). And they may recognize in the phrase an allusion to God's promise of a new covenant with Israel in Jeremiah 31:31–34. However, they will probably be surprised to find that the new covenant theme is rare in both Testaments—except in Hebrews. Here the Greek word for "covenant" and/or "testament" (*diatheke*) is frequent, and sometimes appears in tandem with the adjectives first (*prote*) and new (*kaine*). Indeed, almost half of Hebrews 8 is devoted to the quotation of Jeremiah 31:31–34 (in 8:8b–12) and a concluding interpretive comment: "In speaking of 'a new covenant,' he has made the first one obsolete. And what is obsolete and growing old will soon disappear" (8:13).

In *The New Covenant in Hebrews* (1990), **Susanne Lehne** investigates the role of the covenant in Hebrews from the standpoints of the author and of his first readers. Much of her study is devoted to tracing the new covenant tradition in works other that Hebrews in order to gain perspective on how it functions in Hebrews. After sketching the theme in the Old Testament (with reference to the Patriarchs, Moses, David, and Jeremiah), she notes that apart from some Qumran texts (the *Damascus Document* and the *Pesher on Habakkuk*) the new covenant idea is generally absent from Second Temple Jewish texts. Within the New

Testament, apart from the Last Supper texts, the concept is prominent only in Paul's letters. But in neither the Qumran texts nor the Pauline passages does it have the same meaning as in Hebrews.

What then does new covenant mean in Hebrews? According to Lehne, the concept plays an important "balancing" role in two ways: (1) By creatively reinterpreting the category of covenant from a cultic perspective, the author is able to depict the Christ-event in continuity with and as the perfect fulfillment of the cultic heritage of Israel. (2) By stressing the elements of newness and drawing a contrast to the former system, he succeeds in presenting Christ as the permanent, definitive, superior replacement of that same heritage.

The keywords here are "continuity," "contrast," and "superior," since they express what Lehne regards as fundamental to the author's approach throughout Hebrews not only to the covenant but also to the priesthood, sacrificial cult, and other Old Testament institutions. This approach of continuity, contrast, and superiority in turn guides the author's presentations of revelation (Christian interpretation of the Scriptures), the priesthood of Christ and his sacrificial offering of himself, and Christian life understood as a life of service through communal worship, praise, and confession of God along with works of love, mutual support, and sharing of suffering.

Lehne also regards the new covenant as central to the author's pastoral strategy in advising and encouraging the community that he addresses. To those who were discouraged by persecution and lacked trust, he offered the assurance that Christ has already arrived in the heavens at the end of the path to be traveled by his followers. To those with nostalgia for Jewish cultic institutions, he showed that while the Christ-event derives from scriptural and priestly roots, it was the only sacrifice that could really bring about the access to God that the Old Testament sacrifices sought. Lehne concludes that though Hebrews does not represent a clear rupture with Judaism, with the New Testament it does move furthest in the direction of the break with Judaism that was to take place later.

A novel and synthetic treatment to Hebrews can be found in **Marie E. Isaacs**'s *Sacred Space: An Approach to the Theology of the Epistle to the Hebrews* (1992). She defines "sacred space" as the place that "the worshipper wishes to approach in order to gain access to the deity" (p. 61). She interprets Hebrews as an early Christian attempt to help Jewish Christians to cope with the loss of the Jerusalem Temple in 70 CE and to recognize that they did not need it anymore. She views Hebrews as a reinterpretation of Judaism's established means of access to God by replacing them with Christ and relocating sacred space in heaven—understood as the presence of God.

Sacred space, according to Isaacs, is an area in which God and humankind can meet. For the author of Hebrews, Christ is the prototype of the Torah and the key to Israel's Scriptures as a whole, and only in the light of Christ and with reference to Christ does their true meaning emerge. Likewise, the rest that ancient Israel sought in the promised land of Canaan is to be found only with Christ in heaven. An important purpose of Hebrews is to move readers away from understanding the sacrificial system as an essential part of maintaining contact with God and toward accepting Jesus' death and exaltation as its replacement. While working within the system of ancient Israel, the author transforms it. At best the previous means of access to God were intended to provide a foretaste or preview of better things to come. Even the holy city of Jerusalem (Mount Zion) was but an anticipation of the real sacred space—which is heaven itself.

The author of Hebrews treats the post-mortem fate of Jesus in terms of exaltation. Drawing on Psalm 110:1 ("The Lord says to my lord, 'Sit at my right hand'"), the prologue (1:1–4) interprets Jesus' death as the sacrifice that gained him entry into heaven's sacred territory. Heaven is the place where now the exalted Christ exercises his sovereignty. And heaven is the eschatological goal of the people of God. The goal of their pilgrimage is the reign of God, which Jesus now shares and which he holds out to his followers as their inheritance. Hebrews begins and ends with Christ in heaven as the real sacred space.

Hebrews is a long reflection on Jesus as the definitive means of access to God, and so it compares and contrasts him with Israel's principal mediators who went before him. Despite all his greatness Moses remains only a servant within God's household (heaven), whereas Christ as the Son of God exercises authority over God's household. The priesthood of Aaron and Levi, though previously regarded as permanent, has been abrogated and replaced by the priesthood of Melchizedek that Christ has brought to perfection. And so also the old place of worship (the tabernacle and the Jerusalem Temple) has been superseded and replaced. This is so because in his death and exaltation Jesus has come into the very presence of God—something that the previous high priests failed to do. While the angels are located where Jesus is now (in heaven), their occupation of the same sacred space does not mean that they have equal status with the Son.

Hebrews is accurately described as an extended meditation on the soteriological implications of the suffering and death of Jesus. Moreover, it appears that the early Christians addressed in Hebrews were themselves in a situation that involved suffering (see especially 10:32–34 and 13:3). This theme reaches a high point in 12:1–13 when the author directly considers the sufferings of Christ (12:1–3) and the sufferings of the addressees (12:4–13).

How these sufferings are interpreted is the focus of **N. Clayton Croy**'s *Endurance in Suffering: Hebrews 12:1–13 in its Rhetorical, Religious, and Philosophical Context* (1998). Croy investigates this text in the light of its Jewish and Greco-Roman backgrounds and emphasizes three aspects of the author's understanding of suffering: suffering as an athletic contest *(agon)*, the paraenetic use of exemplars of suffering, and suffering as a divine discipline. He argues that in Hebrews 12:1–13 the author called upon the rhetorical, religious, and philosophical currents of his day to address a community whose primary needs were endurance in faith and fidelity to the confession that had originally constituted the group. He denies that this text supports a punitive view of suffering.

Croy contends that in Hebrews 12:1–3 the sufferings of Christ are portrayed not so much as a martyrdom but more as part of an athletic struggle or contest—as a foot race in particular—with the help of various allusions: "let us also lay aside every weight…and let us run with perseverance the race that is set before us, looking to Jesus the pioneer and perfecter of our faith." The Greek word *prodromos* (pioneer) means literally "the one who runs ahead," and *teleiotes* (perfecter) can be rendered "the one who finishes, or reaches the goal." With this athletic imagery the author joins many Jewish and Greco-Roman writers who used such language in their moral exhortations. Thus he presents Jesus as an agonistic exemplar for Christian life, as the supreme athlete who (alone) has successfully completed the course and now serves as a model to believers. In running his race, Jesus shows endurance and joy in the face of shame and hostility. He has completed the course in advance of all others.

The advice directed especially to the addressees in 12:4–13 focuses on the educational or formative value of suffering, suffering as a discipline (*paideia* in Greek). The question here is whether their suffering should be regarded as punitive (just punishment for sins) or as nonpunitive (an occasion for learning and personal growth). Croy provides a full dossier of ancient Jewish and Greco-Roman texts concerning the causes of suffering and the various interpretations of suffering. He shows that among Jewish and Greco-Roman writers both approaches—punitive and nonpunitive—are well represented.

Croy argues that in Hebrews 12:4–13 the author does not assume that the addressees were being punished for their sins. Rather they are undergoing a process like the discipline that is needed to turn children into mature and responsible adults. The author interprets their present suffering as instruction and discipline in their relationship with God and urges them to submit to

God's instruction and be confident that their doing so will have positive effects. In making his case the author even transforms the punitive approach to suffering suggested in Proverbs 3:11–12 (quoted in Heb 12:5–6) into a formative and educational experience of suffering as divine discipline in this instance.

In the New Testament the word "faith" *(pistis)* has a wide range of meanings, from the basic human sense of trust and steadfastness to theologically focused expressions such as "faith in Christ." In *Faith in Hebrews: Analysis within the Context of Christology, Eschatology, and Ethics* (2001), **Victor (Sung-Yul) Rhee** contends that in Hebrews, faith is intimately related to the Christ-event, and that Christ is not only the model of faith but also the object of faith.

In the spectrum of scholarly approaches to faith in Hebrews, Rhee represents a maximalist position. Some scholars admit only an ethical sense; that is, steadfast endurance in the face of suffering. Others treat faith in an eschatological context; that is, faith as forward-looking with respect to the future and in the present displaying endurance, hope, and confidence in God's promises. Still others emphasize Christ as the model of faith; that is, the one who showed us all how to live in hope even in the midst of suffering. Without ignoring the data in Hebrews on which these various positions are founded, Rhee wants to prove that throughout Hebrews Christ is also and especially the object of faith. While the author of Hebrews does not use Paul's explicit terminology, his Christology, according to Rhee, is close to Paul's emphasis on Christ as the object of faith. This christological approach is foundational for the (mainly temporal) eschatological and ethical approaches in Hebrews.

The core of Rhee's work consists in demonstrating that the christological understanding of faith is present in all the major parts of Hebrews. By building upon and modifying the literary outlines proposed by Albert Vanhoye and others, Rhee regards the main part of Hebrews as consisting of alternating sections of doctrinal exposition and exhortation. He maintains that in every case the christological focus of each exposition provides the basis for the paraenesis that follows.

In this framework Rhee discerns five major parts in Hebrews: the exposition about Christ's divinity (1:1–14) and the exhortation not to drift away (2:1–4); the exposition about Christ's humanity (2:5–18) and the exhortation to enter God's rest (3:1—4:16); the exposition about Christ the merciful high priest (5:1–10) and the exhortation not to fall away (5:11—6:20); the exposition about Christ as the superior high priest (7:1—10:18) and the warning not to live in sin (10:19–39); and the exposition about enduring faith reaching its goal in Jesus (11:1–40) and the exhortation about the danger of rejecting God's word (12:1–29). Rhee concludes that "the characteristics of faith set forth by the author needs to be interpreted in the context of Christology and eschatology to have a proper understanding of faith as intended by the author" (p. 253).

Evaluation

Even though the author of Hebrews is arguably one of the great theologians of the New Testament, he is seldom acknowledged as such. The problem comes from the apparent foreignness of his work, manifest especially in his subtle use of the Scripture and his emphasis on the theological category of sacrifice. Many modern readers find Hebrews puzzling and confusing. In recent years, however, there have been several solid monographs on aspects of the author's theological vision and one fine synthesis (Lindars) that might help to put Hebrews back on the theological map. Much work remains to be done on the theology of Hebrews, and the books covered in this chapter constitute a good start.

Barnabas Lindars' overview of the theology of Hebrews stands among the best and most important modern books on

Hebrews. It came from a learned and mature scholar who understood well what makes Hebrews work on the theological level and who placed its distinctive theology in the wider context of early Christianity and of theology today.

The theme of the wandering people of God in Hebrews 3—4 is in large part the biblical basis for the pilgrim people of God ecclesiology that has a prominent place in Vatican II's Dogmatic Constitution on the Church *(Lumen gentium)*. Even though the historical foundations of Ernst Käsemann's classic monograph on the topic are questionable, no one can doubt the abiding theological significance of his work. The goal of the people's wandering is rest. Jon Laansma looks back to the Old Testament and explores the biblical roots of the concept of rest and compares how the theme is treated by Matthew and the author of Hebrews. Judith Wray not only attends to the biblical background but also traces the trajectory of the concept into the second-century gnostic *Gospel of Truth*.

The monographs on priesthood and sacrifice break new ground with their common focus on the relationship between Christ and Christian life. Since the Protestant Reformation the treatment of these topics in Hebrews has always had as background the theological controversies over the ministerial priesthood and the sacrifice of the Mass, two issues not explicitly discussed in Hebrews. The welcome shift in perspective has the advantage of focusing on issues that are treated in Hebrews and can in fact lead to common ground in dealing with the traditional theological controversies.

In showing how Hebrews understands all Christians as "proleptic priests," John Scholer catches the drift of the "already/not yet" eschatology of Hebrews and highlights the significance of Christ's priesthood and sacrifice for all Christians. Likewise, John Dunnill shows that what the sacrificial system of the Old Testament intended has reached its goal *(telos)* in Christ, and that now all Christians can participate in the uniquely effective sacrifice of Christ in their everyday lives.

And Darrell Pursiful explains how the cultic motif is foundational not only for the spirituality of Hebrews but also for Christian life today, since it helps to root spirituality in the story of Jesus' death and exaltation.

The shift in focus from ministerial priesthood and specific cultic action to Christian life as participation in Christ's priesthood and sacrifice is not only true to the dynamic of Hebrews but it also allows a context in which to view the ministerial priesthood and the Eucharist. The point is that both of these institutions must always be connected directly to Christ's priesthood and sacrifice. The primary analogues are to be found not in the history of religions or even in the Old Testament but rather in the paschal mystery, in the saving significance of Jesus' life, death, and resurrection. Only in this context can we talk meaningfully about Christian priesthood and sacrifice.

The centrality of the paschal mystery in Hebrews is further highlighted by the monographs on "other themes." David Peterson shows that perfection, when applied to Christ, refers to his fulfilling his vocation and reaching his goal (*telos*) and does not imply any previous moral or religious deficiency. Susanne Lehne notes that the new covenant inaugurated by Jesus' death and exaltation stands in a complex relationship of continuity, contrast, and superiority with the old covenant and does not necessitate a full rupture or supersession with regard to Judaism. According to Marie Isaacs, Jesus' death and exaltation open up a new and more perfect sacred space that the Jerusalem temple never offered, the sacred space in heaven where God and humankind meet. For N. Clayton Croy, Christ is the supreme athlete who alone completed the race (*agon*), and the sufferings undergone by those addressed in Hebrews are tests that show the need for discipline, patience, and perseverance. Rhee insists that in Hebrews faith is always related to the Christ-event, and that faith has Christ as both exemplar and object.

Final Thoughts

Where has there been the most progress in the study of Hebrews in recent years? I would list the following five areas of special achievement: the publication of several modern full-scale commentaries in English, the exegetically responsible and spiritually nourishing homiletical expositions by writers who themselves are both exegetes and preachers, the social-science studies that have illumined the situation behind the text, the recognition of the work's rhetorical artistry and of its Christ-centered hermeneutic of the Old Testament, and the realization that all its great theological themes derive from the paschal mystery and serve as commentary on the early Christian confession that "Christ died for our sins in accordance with the scriptures" (1 Cor 15:3).

What areas might be especially fruitful for further research in the future? Besides further research on the many topics opened up over the past thirty years (the historical and literary mysteries of Hebrews, the use of the Old Testament, and theological themes), five topics that come to my mind are the Christology of Hebrews with its equally strong emphasis on the humanity and the divinity of Christ, how the theology of sacrifice in Hebrews fits (or does not fit) with René Girard's theories about violence and the sacred, the roots of the Christian priesthood in the paschal mystery, the significance of Hebrews for Christian-Jewish relations (supersessionist or not?), and the contributions of Hebrews to a Christian theology of suffering.

Of the many books covered in this survey, which ones do I regard as the most helpful? Hebrews is a difficult text, and books on Hebrews also tend to be difficult. Moreover, most of these books originated as doctoral dissertations, and so such works are generally not easy reading for nonspecialists. Without intending to slight any author's hard work on all the books covered in this book, I would list the following as what I regard as the five best and most helpful: Donald A. Hagner, *Encountering the Book of Hebrews* (a sound introduction for the general public); Craig R.

Koester, *Hebrews* (a comprehensive and up-to-date commentary); Barnabas Lindars, *The Theology of the Letter to the Hebrews* (a fine synthesis by a learned biblical scholar); Thomas G. Long, *Hebrews* (a lively exposition that shows the author of Hebrews to be a master preacher and offers wonderful insights for preachers today); and David Peterson, *Hebrews and Perfection* (a fresh treatment of a difficult and important theme).

Bibliography

(The numbers after "Pp." at the end of each item refer to the pages in this volume where the work is treated.)

Anderson, David R. *The King-Priest of Psalm 110 in Hebrews.* Studies in Biblical Literature 21. New York: Peter Lang, 2001. Pp. 59–60.

Attridge, Harold W. *The Epistle to the Hebrews: A Commentary on the Epistle to the Hebrews.* Hermeneia. Philadelphia: Fortress, 1989. Pp. 5–7.

Bateman, Herbert W. *Early Jewish Hermeneutics and Hebrews 1:5–13: The Impact of Early Jewish Exegesis on the Interpretation of a Significant New Testament Passage.* American University Studies VII.193. New York: Peter Lang, 1997. Pp. 55–57.

Cosby, Michael R. *The Rhetorical Composition and Function of Hebrews 11 in Light of Example Lists in Antiquity.* Macon, GA: Mercer University Press, 1988. Pp. 32–33.

Craddock, Fred B. "The Letter to the Hebrews," in *The New Interpreter's Bible,* Vol. XII, pp. 1–173. Nashville: Abingdon, 1998. Pp. 13–15.

Croy, N. Clayton. *Endurance in Suffering: Hebrews 12:1–13 in its Rhetorical, Religious, and Philosophical Context.* Society of New Testament Studies Monograph Series 98. Cambridge: Cambridge University Press, 1998. Pp. 82–84.

D'Angelo, Mary Rose. *Moses in the Letter to the Hebrews.* Society of Biblical Literature Dissertation Series 42. Missoula: Scholars Press, 1979. Pp. 45–46.

Demarest, Bruce. *A History of Interpretation of Hebrews 7,1–10 from the Reformation to the Present.* Beiträge zur Geschichte der biblischen Exegese 19. Tübingen: Mohr (Paul Siebeck), 1976. Pp. 46–48.

deSilva, David A. *Despising Shame: Honor Discourse and Community Maintenance in the Epistle to the Hebrews.* Society of Biblical Literature Dissertation Series 152. Atlanta: Scholars Press, 1995. Pp. 24–26.

deSilva, David A. *Perseverance in Gratitude: A Socio-Rhetorical Commentary on the Epistle "to the Hebrews."* Grand Rapids: Eerdmans, 2000. P. 26.

Dey, Lala Kalyan Kumar. *The Intermediary World and Patterns of Perfection in Philo and Hebrews.* Society of Biblical Literature Dissertation Series 25. Missoula: Scholars Press, 1975. Pp. 19–20.

Dunnill, John. *Covenant and Sacrifice in the Letter to the Hebrews.* Society of New Testament Studies Monograph Series 75. Cambridge: Cambridge University Press, 1992. Pp. 73–75.

Eisenbaum, Pamela M. *The Jewish Heroes of Christian History: Hebrews 11 in Literary Context.* Society of Biblical Literature

Dissertation Series 156. Atlanta: Scholars Press, 1997. Pp. 53–55.

Feld, Helmut. *Der Hebräerbrief.* Erträge der Forschung 228. Darmstadt: Wissenschaftliche Buchgesellschaft, 1985. P. 3.

Gheorghita, Radu. *The Role of the Septuagint in Hebrews.* Wissenschaftliche Untersuchungen zum Neuen Testament 2/160. Tübingen: Mohr-Siebeck, 2003. Pp. 60–61.

Grässer, Erich. *An die Hebräer.* Evangelisch-Katholischer Kommentar zum Neuen Testament 17/1-3. Zurich: Benziger, 1990-97; Neukirchen-Vluyn: Neukirchener. P. 3.

Guthrie, George H. *Hebrews.* NIV Application Commentary. Grand Rapids: Zondervan, 1998. Pp. 15–16.

Guthrie, George H. *The Structure of Hebrews: A Text-Linguistic Analysis.* Novum Testamentum Supplement 73. Leiden: Brill, 1994; Grand Rapids: Baker, 1998. Pp. 33–35.

Hagner, Donald A. *Encountering the Book of Hebrews: An Exposition.* Grand Rapids: Baker Academic, 2002. Pp. 4–5.

Hoppin, Ruth. *Priscilla's Letter: Finding the Author of the Epistle to the Hebrews.* San Francisco: Christian Universities Press, 1997. Pp. 37–38.

Horton, Fred L. *The Melchizedek Tradition: A Critical Examination of the Sources to the Fifth Century A.D. and in the Epistle to the Hebrews.* Society of New Testament Studies Monograph Series 30. Cambridge: Cambridge University Press, 1976. Pp. 48–50.

Hughes, Graham. *Hebrews and Hermeneutics: The Epistle to the Hebrews as a New Testament example of Biblical Interpretation.* Society of New Testament Studies Monograph Series 36. Cambridge: Cambridge University Press, 1979. Pp. 42–43.

Hurst, Lincoln Douglas. *The Epistle to the Hebrews: Its Background of Thought.* Society of New Testament Studies Monograph Series 65. Cambridge: Cambridge University Press, 1990. Pp. 22–23.

Isaacs, Marie E. *Sacred Space: An Approach to the Theology of the Epistle to the Hebrews.* Journal for the Study of the New Testament Supplement 73. Sheffield, UK: Sheffield Academic Press, 1992. Pp. 81–82.

Johnson, Richard W. *Going Outside the Camp: The Sociological Function of the Levitical Critique in the Epistle to the Hebrews.* Journal for the Study of the New Testament Supplement 209. London—New York: Sheffield Academic Press, 2001. Pp. 26–27.

Käsemann, Ernst. *The Wandering People of God: An Investigation of the Letter to the Hebrews.* Minneapolis: Augsburg, 1984. Pp. 67–68.

Kobelski, Paul. *Melchizedek and Melchiresha.* Catholic Biblical Quarterly Monograph Series 10. Washington, DC: Catholic Biblical Association of America, 1981. Pp. 50–51.

Koester, Craig R. *Hebrews: A New Translation with Introduction and Commentary.* Anchor Bible 36. New York: Doubleday, 2001. Pp. 8–11.

Kraus, Wolfgang. "Neuere Ansätze in der Exegese des *Hebräer-briefes.*" *Verkündigung und Forschung* 48/2 (2003) 65-80. P. 3.

Kurianal, James. *Jesus Our High Priest: Ps 110,4 As the Sub-structure of Heb 5,1–7,28.* European University Studies 23/693. Frankfurt: Peter Lang, 2000. Pp. 57–58.

Laansma, Jon. *'I Will Give You Rest': The Rest Motif in the New Testament with Special Reference to Mt 11 and Heb 3–4.* Wissenschaftliche Untersuchungen zum Neuen Testament 2/98. Tübingen: Mohr-Siebeck, 1997. Pp. 68–70.

Lane, William L. *Hebrews 1–8; Hebrews 9–13.* Word Biblical Commentary 47A-B. Dallas: Word Books, 1991. Pp. 7–8.

Lehne, Susanne. *The New Covenant in Hebrews.* Journal for the Study of the New Testament Supplement 44. Sheffield, UK: Sheffield Academic Press, 1990. Pp. 79–81.

Leschert, Dale F. *Hermeneutical Foundations of Hebrews: A Study in the Validity of the Epistle's Interpretation of Some Core Citations from the Psalms.* National Association of Baptist Professors of Religion Dissertation Series 10. Lewiston, NY: Edwin Mellen Press, 1994. Pp. 43–45.

Levy, David M. *The Tabernacle: Shadows of the Messiah. Its Sacrifices, Services, and Priesthood.* Grand Rapids: Kregel, 2003. Pp. 76–77.

Lindars, Barnabas. *The Theology of the Letter to the Hebrews.* New Testament Theology. Cambridge: Cambridge Univer-sity Press, 1991. Pp. 65–67.

Long, Thomas G. *Hebrews*. Interpretation. Louisville: John Knox Press, 1997. Pp. 11–13.

Peterson, David. *Hebrews and Perfection: An Examination of the Concept of Perfection in the 'Epistle to the Hebrews.'* Society for New Testament Studies Monograph Series 47. Cambridge: Cambridge University Press, 1982. Pp. 77–79.

Pursiful, Darrell J. *The Cultic Motif in the Spirituality of the Book of Hebrews*. Lewiston, NY: Edwin Mellen Press, 1993. Pp. 75–76.

Rhee, Victor (Sung-Yul). *Faith in Hebrews: Analysis within the Context of Christology, Eschatology, and Ethics*. Studies in Biblical Literature 19. New York: Peter Lang, 2001. Pp. 84–85.

Salevao, Iutisone. *Legitimation in the Letter to the Hebrews. The Construction and Maintenance of a Symbolic Universe*. Journal for the Study of the New Testament Supplement 219. London—New York: Sheffield Academic Press, 2002. Pp. 28–30.

Schenck, Kenneth. *Understanding the Book of Hebrews: The Story Behind the Sermon*. Louisville: Westminster John Knox, 2003. Pp. 35–37.

Scholer, John M. *Proleptic Priests: Priesthood in the Epistle to the Hebrews*. Journal for the Study of the New Testament Supplement 49. Sheffield: Sheffield Academic Press, 1991. Pp. 71–73.

Swetnam, James. *Jesus and Isaac: A Study of the Epistle to the Hebrews in the Light of the Aqedah*. Analecta Biblica 94. Rome: Biblical Institute Press, 1981. Pp. 51–53.

Thompson, James W. *The Beginnings of Christian Philosophy: The Epistle to the Hebrews*. Catholic Biblical Quarterly Monograph Series 13. Washington, DC: Catholic Biblical Association of America, 1982. Pp. 20–22.

Vanhoye, Albert. *La Lettre aux Hébreux*. Jésus et Jésus-Christ 84. Paris: Desclée, 2001. P. 3.

Vanhoye, Albert. *Structure and Message of the Epistle to the Hebrews*. Subsidia Biblica 12. Rome: Editrice Pontifico Istituto Biblico, 1989. Pp. 30–32.

Wray, Judith Hoch. *Rest as a Theological Metaphor in the Epistle to the Hebrews and the Gospel of Truth: Early Christian Homiletics of Rest*. Society of Biblical Literature Dissertation Series 166. Atlanta: Scholars Press, 1998. Pp. 70–71.

Other Books in This Series

What are they saying about Papal Primacy?
  by J. Michael Miller, C.S.B.

What are they saying about Matthew?
  by Donald Senior, C.P.

What are they saying about Matthew's Sermon on the Mount?
  by Warren Carter

What are they saying about Luke?
  by Mark Allan Powell

What are they saying about Acts?
  by Mark Allan Powell

What are they saying about the Ministerial Priesthood?
  by Rev. Daniel Donovan

What are they saying about Scripture and Ethics?
(Revised and Expanded Ed.)
  by William C. Spohn

What are they saying about Unbelief?
  by Michael Paul Gallagher, S.J.

What are they saying about Environmental Ethics?
  by Pamela Smith

What are they saying about the Formation of Pauline Churches?
  by Richard S. Ascough

What are they saying about the Trinity?
  by Anne Hunt

What are they saying about the Formation of Israel?
  by John J. McDermott

What are they saying about the Parables?
  by David Gowler

What are they saying about Theological Reflection?
  by Robert L. Kinast

Other Books in This Series

What are they saying about Paul and the Law?
by Veronica Koperski

What are they saying about the Pastoral Epistles?
by Mark Harding

What are they saying about Catholic Ethical Method?
by Todd A. Salzman

What are they saying about New Testament Apocalyptic?
by Scott M. Lewis, S.J.

What are they saying about Environmental Theology?
by John Hart

What are they saying about the Catholic Epistles?
by Philip B. Harner

What are they saying about Mark?
by Daniel J. Harrington, S.J.